THE SEBEI

A Study in Adaptation

by

WALTER GOLDSCHMIDT

University of California, Los Angeles

HOLT, RINEHART AND WINSTON

NEW YORK   CHICAGO   SAN FRANCISCO   PHILADELPHIA
MONTREAL   TORONTO   LONDON   SYDNEY
TOKYO   MEXICO CITY   RIO DE JANEIRO   MADRID

DT
433.245
S24
G65
1986

Library of Congress Cataloging-in-Publication Data

Goldschmidt, Walter Rochs, 1913–
  The Sebei.

  (Case studies in cultural anthropology)
  Bibliography: p.
  Includes index.
  1. Sapiny (African people)   I. Title. II. Series.
DT433.245.S24G65   1986   305'.09676'1   85–31718

ISBN 0-03-008922-0

Holt, Rinehart and Winston
The Dryden Press
Saunders College Publishing

Foreword

ABOUT THE SERIES

These case studies in cultural anthropology are designed to bring to students, in beginning and intermediate courses in the social sciences, insights into the richness and complexity of human life as it is lived in different places. They are written by men and women who have lived in the societies they write about and who are professionally trained as observers and interpreters of human behavior. The authors are also teachers, and in writing their books they have kept the students who will read them foremost in their minds. We believe that when an understanding of ways of life very different from one's own is gained, abstractions and generalizations about social structure, cultural values, subsistence techniques, and the other universal categories of human social behavior become meaningful.

ABOUT THE AUTHOR

Walter Goldschmidt is professor emeritus of Anthropology and Psychiatry at the University of California, Los Angeles, where he has taught since 1946. He visited the Sebei three times (1954, 1961–1962, and 1972) and has written three books about them (see bibliography) as well as numerous articles. In addition to his research on the Sebei, he studied the cultures of Indian tribes in California and Alaska and engaged in detailed research on the modern California agricultural community as a staff member of the Bureau of Agricultural Economics, U.S. Department of Agriculture. In all his research he has been accompanied and aided by his wife, Gale.

Goldschmidt has written two books on anthropological theory, *Man's Way*, which develops an evolutionary perspective on culture, and *Comparative Functionalism,* which shows how institutions are responsive to the problems of human collaboration. The theses in these two books underlie the perspective developed in the present work. He is also the author of a textbook, *Exploring the Ways of Mankind*, developed from a series of radio shows on social anthropology he prepared for the National Association of Educational Broadcasters.

The author has been president of the American Anthropological Association, the American Ethnological Society, the Southwestern Anthropological Association, and the Anthropological Film Research Institute; he also was a founding Executive Board member of the African Studies Association. He served as editor of the *American Anthropologist* and was founding coeditor of the journal *Ethos*, now published by the Society for Psychological Anthropology.

Goldschmidt is currently working on the nature of individual careers in tribal societies, which he sees as a dynamic element in the formulation of social institutions, ideas that are expressed in the concluding chapter of this book.

ABOUT THE BOOK

This case study of the Sebei of Uganda is at one and the same time an intimate examination of their culture and a demonstration of the process of evolutionary adaptation. It is both ethnography and theory.

The Sebei are heir to an ancient pastoral tradition that is found throughout the semi-arid lands of East Africa. Some centuries ago they found their way to the well-watered slopes of Mount Elgon where they were living when first discovered at the close of the nineteenth century and where they live today. The new environment created new opportunities and made new demands. They gradually shifted from their old nomadic cattle-keeping, pastoral way of life to one of an increasingly settled, concentrated horticultural production. Goldschmidt shows us how this basic historical change in economy had repercussions throughout the fabric of Sebei social life.

Those Sebei who live in the drier parts of their territory retain much of the old pastoral economy, making it possible to understand what the differences between pastoralism and horticulture mean at a more personal level. The detailed examination of two villages, one pastoral and one horticultural, gives a second way of seeing cultural adaptation, for Goldschmidt insists that we can understand changes only by looking at how they effect the daily lives of the people themselves.

Consider how cattle are intertwined with the social lives of the pastoralists. While the animals constitute an economic resource, their importance to social relationships is far greater. Used in brideprice, adjudication, and exchanges, they are an essential element in every significant social transaction.

Thus, when a cattle owner looks at his herd he does not merely see them as wealth, but as a résumé of his life. He sees cattle as lineages, just as he sees people in terms of lineages; he sees them also as individuals with their own idiosyncracies as he knows his fellow men. But he also sees them as social relationships. Here is an animal obtained from his sister's brideprice; there a cow he got in favorable exchange with a man, whom he therefore addresses as "my kin of the cow"; here are the ones he allocated to his junior wife; there another he dedicated to the spirits to cure his ailing senior wife, and so on. His herd is a kind of template for his own social history—and if it is a large one it shows how successfully he has conducted his affairs.

For Sebei farmers, land replaces cattle in their hierarchy of values and they have adapted many of their laws of stock ownership to the control of land as a form of property. But land is not like cattle and the *social* meanings have largely been lost. This is but an example of the way that changes in the intimate life of the Sebei have been affected by the transition from pastoralism to farming.

In such ways, Goldschmidt relates the intimacies of social life to a theoretical understanding of social change. More particularly, institutional change is seen as coming about through the altered pattern of individual choices of action because new ecological conditions have created new options and new priorities. Central to this position is the recognition that tribal peoples have *careers*, and that career choices transform social institutions.

Goldschmidt was accompanied in his field studies by his wife, Gale, who contributed most of the excellent pictures as well as much of the detail of Sebei social life. They lived for most of two years in close contact with the Sebei, which has enabled them to make this lively and intimate study.

Students will find this book compelling, clear, and intriguing because of the lively style of presentation and the evocation of the feelings as well as the understandings of the Sebei—often in their own comments and verbatim bits of their conversations.

Instructors will find the work useful as an example of pastoral life and as a representation of African culture. They will also find it useful in dealing with such theoretical matters as cultural evolution, ecological adaptation, the interconnectedness of cultural elements, and the relationship between the individual and his or her culture.

GEORGE AND LOUISE SPINDLER
Series Editors
Calistoga, California

Preface

Some twenty-five years ago, shortly after I returned from my first visit to the Sebei, George Spindler invited me to write a book for the Holt Case Studies series that he and his wife, Louise, had just begun. I was pleased to be asked. I felt like a godfather to the series, since he had been my teaching assistant at UCLA a decade earlier, in which I had each student read several monographs. Spin saw the value of such readings, but also realized that the works available were not written for undergraduates. His prescience has paid off in the rich literature of the Spindler series.

After long deliberation, I declined the Spindlers' invitation for one simple reason: I did not yet understand the Sebei. Why did I feel uncertain about these people, among whom my wife and I had just spent an exciting and informative six months? I concluded that I did not understand them because they were so varied, differing from one part of their territory to another, that they were in fact a people in transition. Not transition into the Western world (though that is also a part of the picture) but in transition from one kind of economy—cattle pastoralism—to another—hoe cultivation of plantains (bananas) and maize (corn). This shift can be seen both in space and time, for some Sebei retained much of the old pastoralist pattern while others completely altered their economy.

These ruminations about my own ignorance led me to undertake a major research project (supported by the National Science Foundation and the National Institutes of Mental Health) to investigate what this shift in economy meant for the attitudes, values, and social organization of the community. This research program—the Culture and Ecology Project—involved the study of four East African tribes that had undergone similar shifts and was made in collaboration with a cultural geographer (Dr. Philip Porter) and a psychological anthropologist (Dr. Robert B. Edgerton) as well as three other ethnographers. This book does not refer to these other tribes, but it does utilize some of the rich information supplied by Porter and Edgerton.

I had in the meantime written a small theoretical treatise on cultural evolution (*Man's Way*) and I saw the investigation of this shift as an example of the evolutionary process. Let's stop for a moment to give some thought to what cultural evolution means, for it is these ideas that illuminate the Sebei scene, and I will return to them at the close.

Cultural Evolution   The idea of *cultural* evolution is an analogy to *biological* evolution. In biological evolution we tend to look at what I call the Grand Scheme—that remarkable historical emergence of ever higher, more complex, and more differentiated forms of life. But if we look at the *process* of evolution, we realize that this Grand Scheme is a secondary result of something quite different. The process of evolution lies in the continuous and ordinary events of life forms acquiring new capacities that make them better able to cope with their environment, those getting these traits surviving and those less able falling by the wayside—the process of natural selection that was formulated by Charles Darwin in *Origin of Species*. This continual pattern of adjustment in the form and function of life forms constitutes the process of biological evolution.

The idea of cultural evolution has as long a history as the idea of biological evolution. Most discussion of cultural evolution is about the Grand Scheme type of development. First hunters and gatherers with their small bands, then horticulturists and pastoralists with their clans, and finally agriculturists with their states—or some such schema. Of course, there has been such an evolutionary progression in the long sweep of human history, but it tells us nothing about how the changes took place, of what goes on in the process of evolutionary development. We must remember also that cultural evolution is *like* biological evolution, but it is by no means the same. We must be careful to consider what is similar and what is different:

> In biological evolution, new traits come from *genetic mutations*; in cultural evolution, they are *discoveries, inventions,* or *ideas*.
>
> In biological evolution, these traits must be transmitted *genetically* to offspring and only become general in the population over a long period of time; in cultural evolution, they are transmitted by *learning*, and they can spread rapidly through a community.
>
> In biological evolution, the role of the individual is *passive*, it either has or does not have the gene; in cultural evolution, the individual is *active* and, in fact, persons can decide that a change is desirable and even induce others to follow it.

There are also some similarities. Both biological evolution and cultural evolution build new traits or abilities on the existing structure of capacities. This change is gradual; it is evolutionary rather than revolutionary, and much of the past always remains in the present. Of course cultural evolution is much faster; it took about five million years for modern humanity to evolve biologically from some apelike ancestors, but only about fifty thousand years (one one-hundredth of the time) for cultural evolution to transform simple bands of hunting and gathering peoples into the complex diverse forms of modern-day society.

Ecology   Anthropologists have adopted another concept from biology that relates to the evolutionary process: *ecology*. Ecology is the interrelationship between any *species* of plant or animal and the environment in which it lives: the climate and soil, the food resources, and the dangers and threats to its existence. In the biological process, the creature inherits the traits through genetic mutation that enable it to cope with that ecological context, so that we may say the life form is shaped by its environment. Of course, each plant and animal is part of the context of all others, as well.

Cultural ecology is the way by which a *community* of people relates to its environment, including the context of other groups of people. This they do with the tools and techniques at their disposal, but also by structuring their attitudes and social relationships in such a way as to perform the tasks necessary to their continued existence. Ecology, or ecological adaptation, is the essential mechanism by which evolutionary change takes place; this is true of cultural evolution as well as biological evolution.

Not all evolution is progressive, but it is all adaptive. When a species finds an ecological niche it may, in one way or another, simplify its system—as with the loss of eyesight among most animals that dwell permanently in caves. Similarly with cultural adaptation. For instance, most scholars believe that pastoralism as a mode of life developed as a kind of offshoot from early civilizations with elaborated political institutions. But as people followed their herds into arid areas, they abandoned the political institutions that could not be supported and reverted to a tribal form of social organization. Yet the long-term and most visible effect of both biological and cultural evolution is the gradual growth in complexity and technical competence that constitutes the Grand Scheme of evolutionary development.

Summary   This book is two things: an examination of Sebei culture as it existed at the time of our research, and a case study in the process of cultural evolution. Note that I am speaking about how the Sebei lived when I did my research there, so that when I say today and use the present tense, it means 1954–1962. In the Epilogue, I will indicate some of the things that have happened to them since then. To understand the Sebei of today, it is necessary to understand the dynamics of this evolutionary process, and, in turn, an examination of the Sebei illuminates this process. We concentrate on what it means to shift from a pattern of life dominated by the need to care for life-sustaining livestock to one dominated by the need to cultivate the soil for a livelihood. This is the process of ecological adaptation; it is not to be viewed as some kind of step up the ladder of Grand Scheme evolution; agricultural Sebei are not superior to pastoral Sebei.

We explore this process by examining two dimensions in the affairs of the Sebei: time and space. Chapters 1 through 3 reconstruct the history of the Sebei transformation in the century or more before the coming of British colonial rule in Uganda. This is the time dimension. Chapters 4 and 5 deal with the differences between two communities, intensely studied in 1962, one in the sector devoted exclusively to horticulture, the other in which pastoral pursuits retain a major role in economic life. This is the space dimension. Chapters 6 and 7 on religious rituals also illuminate both the historical and the contemporary differences. In the final chapter we will draw together the information to return to what Sebei life tells us about the process of evolutionary adaptation.

Acknowledgments

First and foremost, I want to express my appreciation to the people of Sebei, to Psiwa Kapchemesyekin, to Salimu arap Kambuya, Andyema arap Kambuya, Ndiwa arap Kambuya, and to all the others who, directly and indirectly, helped me to gain some insight into their manner of life. Their friendship sustained me when we were among them and remains a source of personal satisfaction.

Second, I want to thank my colleagues who worked with me on the Culture and Ecology Project; particularly Robert B. Edgerton and Philip W. Porter who worked with me among the Sebei, but also Francis Conant, Symmes C. Oliver, and Edgar V. Winans who helped to formulate the project as a whole. Most important among these colleagues was my wife, Gale, who shared our Sebei experiences, gathered much valuable information, and took many of the photographs that appear in these pages.

Third, I acknowledge by debt to the diverse agencies that over the years have supported one or another part of the research on which this book is based: the Fulbright program, the Social Science Research Council, the Wenner-Gren Foundation, the National Institutes of Mental Health (P.H.S. Grant MH-04097), the National Science Foundation (Grant G11713), and the Academic Senate of the University of California at Los Angeles.

Fourth, I express my appreciation to the University of California Press (and to Robert Edgerton) for permission to quote from *The Individual in Cultural Adaptation, A Study of Four East African Peoples* (U. of Calif. Press, 1971). The passages quoted are from pages 105–107 and 119–120.

Finally, I thank Daniel Kerman and Martin Cohen, who helped me in preparing this manuscript, and Philip Porter and Patrick Finnerty, who prepared the maps.

Table of Contents

Foreword   iii

Preface   vi

Acknowledgments   ix

List of Illustrations   xii

1   The Landscape: Natural and Cultural   1
    The Pastoral Tradition in East Africa   1
    Mount Elgon as the Sebei Habitat   3
    Basic Changes in Sebei Ecology   10

2   The Cultural Heritage   13
    Economic Elements   13
    Social Organization   16
    The Social Uses of Livestock   18
    Age Sets and Initiation   21
    Territorial Organization   25
    Summary   26

3   The Transformation of Sebei Society   27
    Sedentarization   27
    The Organization of Warfare   29
    The Creation of Community Law   30
    Changes in the Domestic Scene   32
    The Changing Pattern of Sebei Careers   34
    The Coming of External Control   34

4   Sasur: The Farming Community   39
    The Research Program   39
    Households and Household Tasks   40
    Land in Sasur   48
    Ritual Adaptation   52
    Family Relationships   54
    Marriage   55
    Illness and Oaths   62
    Death and Funerals   66

5   Kapsirika: The Livestock Community   71
    Household Domestic Economy   73
    Cattle Exchanges   76

Negotiations at a Funeral   80
Witchcraft and Family Relations   89
Warfare   91
The Kapsirika Community   93

6   Circumcision   95
Preparation for Initiation   96
The Ceremony of Cutting   97
"Crying the Knife"   102
Later Rituals   105
Variation in the Circumcision Rite   108
The Continuing Tradition of Circumcision   110

7   Religion   113
Sebei-Wide Rituals   114
Clan Rites   116
Twins and Other Special Children   117
Rites of Passage   121
Domestic Rites   122
Oathing and Witchcraft   124
The General Character of Sebei Religion   124
Sebei Ethos   126

8   The Process of Adaptation   129
An Overview of the Change Process   129
Prehistoric Adaptation   130
The Process of Historic Change   132
Ecological Adaptations   134
Institutional Diversity   138
Conflict and Institutional Response   140
Anomie and the Evolutionary Process   144
A Model for Evolutionary Change   145
Change as the Human Condition   149

Epilogue   151
Readings   155
Glossary   157
Index   161

List of Illustrations

Map 1   The Sebei and their neighbors   xiii
Map 2   Block diagram of Sebei territory   4–5
Photo 1   Landscape near Sasur   6
Photo 2   Air view of Kapsirika   9
Photo 3   Child playing a pretend game   13
Photo 4   A highly prized bull   19
Photo 5   A boy soon to be circumcised   23
Photo 6   The same boy after circumcision   24
Photo 7   A Sebei warrior in 1890   35
Photo 8   Our house in Sasur   41
Photo 9   Household scene   42
Photo 10   A child caretaker   43
Photo 11   A work party   45
Photo 12a   Drinking beer   46
Photo 12b   Women drinking beer at a ceremony   47
Photo 13   Pouring a libation of beer   53
Photo 14   Bargaining the bridesprice   59
Photo 15   Mock fight   61
Photo 16   Removing a curse   64
Photo 17   Our camp in Kapsirika   72
Photo 18   Drying grain   74
Photo 19   Milking   75
Photo 20   Bleeding a bullock   77
Photo 21a   Examining the cattle herd   82
Photo 21b   Allocating cattle to heirs   83
Photo 22   Initiates learning to dance   98
Photo 23   Initiates being painted   99
Photo 24   Initiates just before circumcision   100
Photo 25   Being circumcised   102
Photo 26   Reaction to crying the knife   103
Photo 27   The girl who cried   104
Photo 28   Painting the initiates   106
Photo 29   The twin ceremony   120

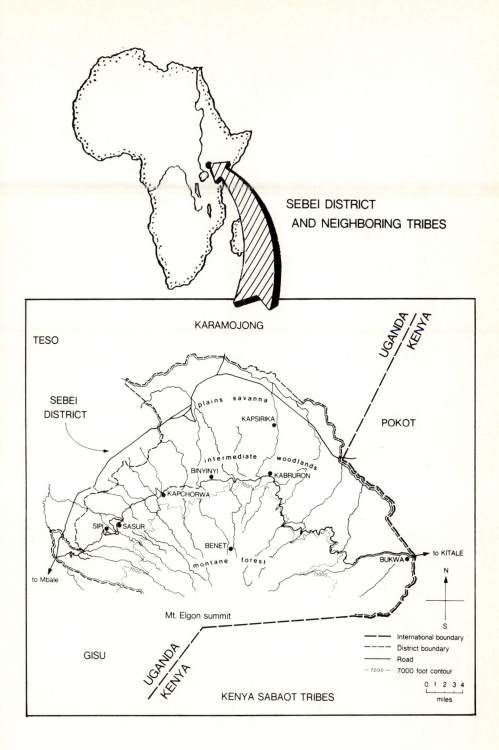

SEBEI DISTRICT
AND NEIGHBORING TRIBES

KARAMOJONG

TESO

SEBEI
DISTRICT

UGANDA
KENYA

POKOT

plains savanna

KAPSIRIKA

intermediate   woodlands

BINYINYI   KABRURON

KAPCHORWA

7000

SIPI   SASUR

BENET

montane   forest   7000

7000

to Mbale

BUKWA   to KITALE

N

S

Mt. Elgon summit

GISU

UGANDA
KENYA

KENYA SABAOT TRIBES

International boundary
District boundary
Road
—7000— 7000 foot contour

0 1 2 3 4
miles

1/The landscape:
Natural and cultural

The Sebei live on the north slope of a giant extinct volcano, Mount Elgon, in Uganda, in the heart of Africa. They belong to a language group known as Kalenjin, which they share with such peoples as the Nandi, Kipsigi, and Pokot of Kenya. They are more distantly related to peoples called Southern Nilotic, who occupy much of the arid high plains extending from the Sudan and Ethiopia to central Tanzania, among whom the best known are the Maasai.

THE PASTORAL TRADITION IN EAST AFRICA

The Sebei are heir to an ancient culture that has its beginning in pre-Christian times and shares generic features with the ancient Semitic tribes described in the Old Testament. The roots of this culture go back some forty centuries. The basic economy of this ancient culture is what anthropologists call *pastoralist*; that is, the people are dependent on raising livestock for food —cattle, sheep, and goats in varying proportions, supplemented in some areas with camels, donkeys, or both. The animals eat the natural grass and foliage, which means that the flocks and herds must be moved to where grass, water, and salt are available. This in turn means that often the people must also move. The amount of movement, whether it is almost daily or only seasonal, depends on local conditions, but they cannot live long in one place before the grass is eaten by their animals. We therefore call them *nomadic pastoralists*. Though nomadism in some degree is always necessary, there are home camps, and most of these Nilotic peoples also engage in some cultivation of crops, originally sorghum and other cereal grasses. The actual mixture and relative importance of livestock and grain varies as local conditions vary, but normally in some degree all these items are part of the basic inventory of economic resources.

While every Nilotic tribe is unique, certain cultural features are general among them. These are features of the ancient ecological adaptation to the semiarid plains environment. In addition to dependence upon livestock, the secondary use of crops, and a nomadic way of life may be added: the importance of both milk and blood (taken from the veins of living cattle) in the

1

diet; the use of wild honey and perhaps also the making of beehives, as well as beer-making from honey or grain; the use of iron for spears and perhaps also hoes, which means also the craft of smithing; and oval leather shields, which suggest that they engaged in warfare. The use of cowrie shells and of copper ornaments are probably later innovations but also widespread among them, as is the making of pottery. In their social organization are also some universal features: the reckoning of descent through the male line and masculine control of cattle (though women milk the cows), polygyny, that is, men being allowed to take several wives, and bride payments in livestock. The people are organized into lineages or clans (patrilineal descent groups whose members consider one another as kin) and these are expected to give mutual support in legal disputes and other confrontations. There are no hereditary chiefs and rarely any real political organization.

Instead, the most characteristic single feature of Southern Nilotic organization is the system of *age sets*. Age sets are formed when youths are initiated at puberty or early manhood; each set bracketing several years. As time goes on, the men in these sets grow older, and a new cadre of youth are initiated into the succeeding age set. It follows that all men belong to one of several age sets that form a kind of hierarchy, with senior elders at the top, followed by junior elders, senior warriors, junior warriors, and the uninitiated boys. The details of this social system vary from tribe to tribe, but everywhere they share these features: (1) the unit age sets are strongly bonded groups of men who owe one another special respect and allegiance; (2) each set moves as a unit from one social status to another with the passage of time; (3) the age set system gives a hierarchical structure based on the principle of age seniority; and (4) men are inducted into the system through initiation in early adulthood, an initiation in which they are indoctrinated with the values of the community and in which the lessons are intensified through the shared pain of physical hazing and circumcision. A counterpart initiation for girls, involving clitoridectomy and often more elaborate operations on the vagina, is found among many of the Southern Nilotic peoples, including the Sebei.

Finally, there is the matter of warfare. The masculine orientation of cattle-keeping peoples is probably associated with the dangers inherent in herding livestock in a landscape where lions, leopards, and other predators constitute an ever-present threat. But livestock is also subject to another kind of predation—raiding by enemy groups. It is for this function that the age-set system, which bonds together the able-bodied young men into collaborative teams, is so important. Such young men will not be content merely to protect their herds from others, but they will also initiate raids themselves. So a pattern of intertribal warfare, normally in the form of localized raids and counter-raids, but capable of escalating to major conflicts, is an important feature of life on the high plains of East Africa.

This ancient culture spread throughout East Africa. It was preceded by two other peoples, a hunting and gathering people generally called Dorobo, remnants of which are still found in remote areas, and a Cushitic population that presumably was more agricultural, a few remnants of which also remain, though what their fate was and why they largely disappeared is a mystery. Meanwhile, the more humid parts of Africa were filled with Bantu-speaking peoples whose culture was adapted to the cultivation of crops and who now occupy most of Africa from the Congo basin southward and also infiltrated the better-watered region of East Africa. As the Nilotic culture spread, it made local adaptations, and where it encountered the usually more humid mountains, it often expanded its agricultural production and paid less attention to livestock. One such area was Mount Elgon, where we now turn.

MOUNT ELGON AS THE SEBEI HABITAT

Sebei-speaking people (*Sabaot*) once occupied the whole of Mount Elgon, separated into a half dozen tribes. The Bantu-speaking people called Gisu pushed them out of the southwest sector of this circle in the mid-nineteenth century, and the colonial boundary between Kenya and Uganda effectively cut the southern group off from the northern. The three tribes occupying the north slope of the mountain and some of the plains below (the Mbai, the Sor, and the Sapiñ, from which the modern name Sebei derives) effectively amalgamated into what we now call the Sebei.

Mount Elgon rises from the plains (which in Uganda are at an elevation of 3000 to 4000 feet) to a height of 14,175 feet. We must look more closely at this mountain, the largest volcanic mountain mass in the world, though not the highest.

A Tour of Sebeiland   I will take you on a tour of it to show you the different kinds of environment it offers. The block diagram (pages 4–5) will help you keep your bearings as we travel across the escarpment and then back across the plains. The diagram is a kind of three-dimensional map, but as we are looking at the mountain from somewhere to the northwest, it is backward with the west to the right and the east to the left. The mountain peak, which is not so high as to be covered with snow, is hidden behind the horizon.

We enter the Sebei country from the town of Mbale (and onto the diagram at the extreme right) on a modern surfaced road. The blacktop was being laid when we were there in 1962, and during the rain the road was often a very trying quagmire. Just before we get to the little town of Muyembe we turn off to the right on a gravel road and soon begin to climb on a steep, but well constructed, road with hairpin turns to Bulegene, in Sebei territory, at an elevation of about 5000 feet. The road now becomes a narrow red strip between lush dark green plantain *shambas* (as the cultivated gardens are called in East Africa) into which the eye can rarely penetrate. The occasional round house with thatched roof and red mud walls (sometimes a cluster of two or three) along the road gives no clue to how densely settled the area is, but there are as many as 700 people per square mile. You might see a few tethered goats but no cattle and few if any granaries.

After two or three miles we start to climb, the road becoming so steep that

I am reminded of the first time I came up it with all my safari gear loaded into a Volkswagen minibus. It slowed down to two miles an hour, but just as I was sure that I would have to stop to off-load baggage we suddenly crested the top. From this crest we can see, about half a mile ahead, the shining corrugated iron roofs of the *dukas*, as East African shops are called, of the town of Sipi. We get an occasional glimpse of the red cliffs or a rare view of the grasslands way up the mountain if they are not clouded with the mists that usually shroud them. We drive past Sipi, turning sharply inward and downward toward the mountain to cross a stream and then switch back outward and up around the next spur, a pattern that will continue as we drive across the escarpment of the mountain along a road that extends about 40 miles to the Kenya border. This first stream is the Sipi River, with its great

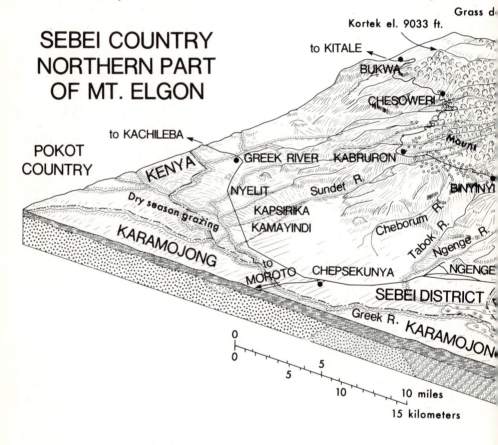

SEBEI COUNTRY
NORTHERN PART
OF MT. ELGON

AN ISOMETRIC
BLOCK DIAGRAM

Vertical exaggeration 1:1.67

Constructed by P. W. Porter and drafted by S. Haas
Department of Geography, University of Minnesota
May, 1975

waterfalls and cascades that are particularly spectacular during the rainy season, and we must stop to get a good view.

A little farther on we come to the village of Sasur, one of the two communities we studied in detail in 1962. Just below the road we had had a house built for us in native fashion called "wattle and daub"—poles set in a circle held together with flexible branches woven between them and then plastered solid with the red mud of the region. Stringers are stretched from the outer poles to the center poles. Our conical roof was thatched so beautifully that it never leaked a drop in one of the wettest years on record (106 inches of rain). It was a lovely house, but very dark even on bright days as the eaves hung low over the wooden windows that had been set in the mud walls. Maunya, from whom we had borrowed the land, received this house as a

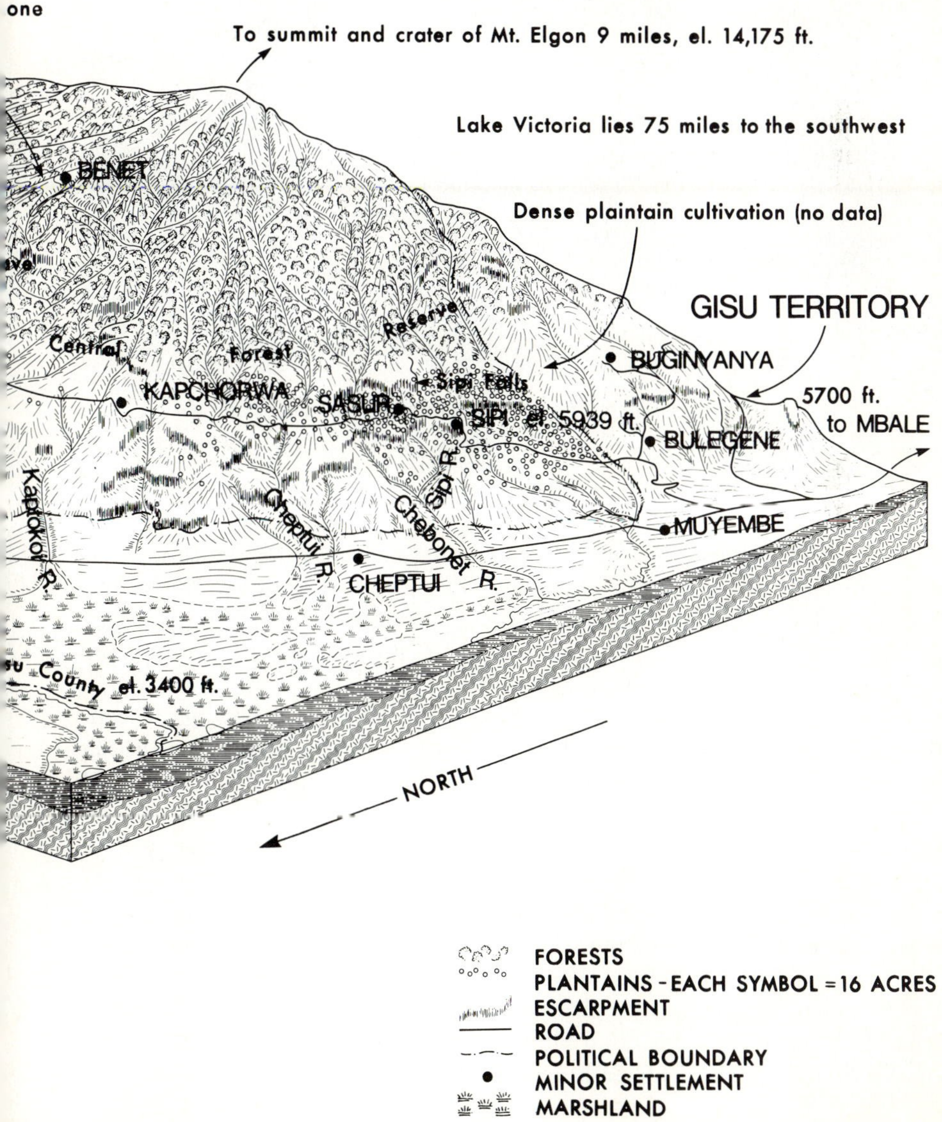

one

To summit and crater of Mt. Elgon 9 miles, el. 14,175 ft.

Lake Victoria lies 75 miles to the southwest

Dense plaintain cultivation (no data)

GISU TERRITORY

BENET

Central   Forest   Reserve

KAPCHORWA   SASUR   Sipi Falls   BUGINYANYA

SIPI el. 5939 ft.   5700 ft.
                      to MBALE

BULEGENE

Kapokoi R.   Cheptui   Chebonet   Sipi R.

MUYEMBE

CHEPTUI R.

su County el. 3400 ft.

NORTH

FORESTS
PLANTAINS - EACH SYMBOL = 16 ACRES
ESCARPMENT
ROAD
POLITICAL BOUNDARY
MINOR SETTLEMENT
MARSHLAND

Photo 1. Landscape near Sasur. In the foreground is a field from which corn had been harvested. To the left of the houses, a coffee field is growing in the middle ground.

kind of rental payment, but unfortunately we cannot see this house now, as it was burned down shortly after Maunya moved in—burned by jealous neighbors, I was told. But we can stop for a view from the rock outcropping and see the plains below, flat as a sea, light green or shimmering with swamp water during the rainy season, tan in the dry season.

We must get away from our many old friends as soon as possible to continue down the red road. It is about eight miles to Kapchorwa, the district headquarters, the capital of Sebei, with its government offices, which in 1954 were still mud and thatch, but which now are made of cement with tile or tin roofs. We must certainly stop to visit the district commissioner, who is the chief administrative officer, appointed by the central government of Uganda. He is probably not a member of the Sebei tribe. In 1954, these officers were British civil servants, but after independence they are Ugandans and were Sebei at Kapchorwa. When we visited in 1972, however, the district commissioner was an army officer appointed by the dictator, Idi Amin. I remember that when I called on him—he obviously knew that I was coming —he took the pistol off his desk and placed it on a shelf behind him, as he welcomed me by my Sebei name, Labu. We became good friends, and I called him by his nickname, Kali-Kali (which means sharp in Swahili). I gave him a copy of my first book on the Sebei before I left.

Beyond Kapchorwa the plantains are rarely seen but only *shambas* of maize and open grassland where small herds of cattle or goats are herded by boys. The houses, though actually fewer in number are easier to see in the open country. They are now more often in clusters, though less well made. Attached to them will be cattle pens or *kraals*, as they are called, and nearby also will be rows of wickerwork granaries, in which the maize and millet are stored. On the way we cross the Atari River. Just beyond is the place where, shortly after our arrival in 1954, we witnessed our first Sebei ritual—the circumcision of five girls. We spent much time at that place watching the cycle of rites over the following months.

We soon arrive at Binyinyi, where we had been headquartered in that first trip, in an about-to-be abandoned government resthouse made of mud and wattle, with only gaps for doors and windows through which nightly we heard the howling of hyenas. That building has long since disappeared. Here we must stop, for Binyinyi is the best takeoff point from which to climb up to Benet. The road we have been traveling since Sipi stays close to the 6000 foot contour; Benet is a two or three hour climb to the 10,000 foot level, through a beautiful bamboo forest with colubus monkeys, bush pigs, and other small game. A few Sebei lived in the forest until the colonial government made everybody move out, but there are people living above it. Halfway up, we stop at the cave of Arkok; it is one of the many caves in this porous volcanic mountain in which the Sebei would hide their cattle, women, and children when being raided by neighboring tribes. This one is particularly famous as the place occupied by a prophet, a religious man who could foretell events.

The area called Benet is rich green grassland surrounded by forests and we see the long rectangular flat-roofed houses at the edge of the woods. They are different from anything we have seen elsewhere in Sebei—or in all of Uganda and Kenya, for that matter. These tightly sealed houses, which the people share with their livestock, are warm against the bitter cold found at this altitude, even though it is almost on the equator. The architectural form is thought to be a heritage from the old Cushitic culture; it was retained by the Sebei because it is so well suited to the climate.

Having returned to Binyinyi, we go on to Kabruron over a landscape that gets more arid, rough, and empty. Kabruron was the end of the road in 1954 and I am told that it is again nearly so, for lack of upkeep. My chief memory of Kabruron was the evening we were among a dozen or so guests of Sir Andrew Cohen, then the governor of Uganda, for a state dinner, with crested china and three glasses at each setting—a dinner that had to be cooked on primus stoves. (The next day the governor and his entourage went on to Bukwa for a holiday of fishing on the Suam River, his plates and dishes loaded on the heads of porters.) At its best, the road beyond Kabruron is difficult, and we must pray that our Landrover will make it over the rugged and almost empty terrain that lies to the east. The view to the north is un-impeded, and we see the plain, a dry sea with the great blue-black Mount Debasien rising out of it like a giant ship. We climb well over 7000 feet before reaching a crest that descends gradually to the town of Bukwa.

Bukwa is the easternmost community of the Sebei, lying on the Suam River that forms the border with Kenya. The houses here are often rectangular and have corrugated iron roofs and sometimes cement slab floors instead of the tamped earth of the traditional houses. Many of the fields are fenced and even in 1954 we saw some of the people using tractors.

We cross the Suam and find our way down a steep and rugged road to get to the plains and pick up the road that leads to the border town of Greek River, a military outpost established about 1914 to control the raiding be-tween the Pokot, whose territory lies to the east, the Karamojong, who occupy the land north of the stream, also called Greek River, and the Sebei. I re-member our first visit there in January 1954 in the company of the district commissioner of Sebei, who was holding a conference with his counterpart officers of the other two districts and the leaders of the three tribes. It was an effort to stop the raiding that was still going on. I retain two memories of that visit. The first was feeling how much more elegant and foppish the Karamojong and the Pokot were than the Sebei, for these two tribes had retained much of their traditional costume as well as the ancient custom of aggressive raids. The second was observing three roosters tethered to a fence-post awaiting their fate as a meal for the three district commissioners. The three chickens were busy establishing their pecking order, and it seemed symbolic of the purpose of the meeting we were attending: three tribes tied down by colonial rule trying to establish their superiority.

We continue westward along the dirt road; no signs of human life are now visible, for the land is quite empty. The raiding that was sporadic in the 1950s and 1960s had become so continuous that the Sebei were driven out of the territory and only the herds of giraffe, zebra, and buck are to be seen.

We cross the Sundet river after a few miles and turn in toward the moun-tain along an obscure track to look for the place in Kapsirika, which was the second village of our 1962 study, where we had had our camp. When we were there then, we would come across herds of a hundred or so cattle grazing on the thin grass tended by the young men and see long narrow fields planted to millet and maize, cultivated by ox-drawn plows. The houses were a half mile or more apart. Usually there would be several together, each belonging to one of the wives, the whole surrounded by a brush fence and this attached to the *kraal* for the cattle. Here there were only 25 persons per square mile. We find the giant thornbush tree where our camp had been, but there is no trace of the house we had built according to the pattern of the Sebei. It was a much poorer house than the one in Sasur, without mudding (for it is good to let the air penetrate) and with only a thin layer of thatch (as there is less rainfall). The annual rainfall is calculated at about 35 inches. Our Kapsirika friends—those who had not been killed in raids—have all moved away, some up on the mountain, some further west where there is a government outpost.

Photo 2. View of Kapsirika from the air, showing the long narrow fields and open grazing land. The larger white circles are houses, the small dots are granaries.

We had visited them on our last trip to the Sebei in 1972, for by then they had all moved out of Kapsirika and the other villages on these dry and open plains. So we find our way back to the road and continue westward to Chepse-kunya, the police station where our Kapsirika friends had settled in 1972, and stop to visit them before getting on the paved road back to Mbale.

General Features of the Landscape We have now completed our circuit and found how varied were the landscapes, both natural and cultural, that constitute the territory of the Sebei. It is possible to divide the highly varied territory into four major zones, created by the differentials in altitude and in rainfall. The prevailing winds are from the west and bring moisture picked up from Lake Victoria, the world's second largest lake, and drop it on the mountainside, so that rainfall is greater in the west and at high altitudes than to the east and at lower altitudes. The four zones are:

1. The western escarpment, extending from the western boundary to Kapchorwa at elevations of 5000 to 7000 feet, which is richly watered and suitable for growing plantains, other food crops, and coffee. It has an annual rainfall of between 60 and 70 inches. (The year we lived there was exceptionally wet.) It has population densities that reach 1000 per square mile and houses over half of the total Sebei population.

2. The northern and eastern escarpment, which has lower rainfall (annual averages between 40 and 50 inches) and lower population densities (mostly under 100 per square mile). It is suitable for growing maize and other grains and for keeping livestock, though there are isolated valleys where plantains and coffee can be grown. It contains about a third of all Sebei.

3. The mountain area above the forest at altitudes between 9000 and 10,000 feet, which has a small population. It is cold and wet; the people raise livestock, especially sheep, and do some farming—mostly of such recently introduced crops as potatoes. Honey is an important product, used for making beer. Less than 5 percent of the population lives here.

4. The plains area, a dry flat land that is most suitable for raising livestock grazing on natural fodder. It is also possible to cultivate grains there. The climate is warm, there is much sunshine and little rain. About 10 percent of the Sebei lived there in 1962.

BASIC CHANGES IN SEBEI ECOLOGY

When the ancestors of the Sebei arrived at Mount Elgon, the climatic features were the same as today, but the cultural features—the crops and animals and houses were not. We believe that this happened some 500 years ago, but nothing is really known about this event. There is little helpful archaeological excavation and the Sebei have no stories or legends about the move. We presume that they replaced a Cushitic population, but there is not much, beyond the rectangular houses in Benet, as evidence. Our interest is, however, in how the changes came to make the cultural landscape what it now is.

Economic Changes Two sets of events that took place well after the arrival of the Sebei-speaking people had a profound effect upon this shift. The first of these had to do with the acquisition of two new crops, corn and plantains. They undoubtedly brought sorghum, millet, and other grains. Maize or Indian corn was brought into Africa through European influence some time after the discovery of America and spread rapidly into the interior, reaching the Sebei long before Europeans arrived. The first variety was not easy to grind and corn did not become popular until a softer variety was introduced, probably late in the nineteenth century.

Plantains, a crop long cultivated by Bantu peoples in the more humid area, was adopted by the Sebei probably early in that century. Plantains are similar to our bananas but are not eaten as we eat this fruit. They are picked when green, peeled, and boiled or steamed and have much the taste and consistency of sweet potatoes. They are therefore a starchy staple food, serving the same dietary function as corn meal in Latin America, wheat and other grains in Europe, or rice in India and the Far East. Where the climate is suitable, they are a very cost-effective crop, able to support the high population density of the Sipi area. Plantains have no viable seeds, but are planted as shoots. The root system spreads underground and sends up trunks, each of which grows to the size of a small tree and produces a single stem of fruit. It takes about two or three years for a plantain *shamba* to yield a harvest, but once it starts it can, if properly tended, continue to produce fruit for 50 years; it can do so virtually year round (especially if different varieties are planted) and it can produce a greater volume of carbohydrates than grains can in Sebei— and with very little labor and without fertilizers or irrigation. These characteristics make it possible for plantains to support not only a dense population, but one permanently settled on the land. We will later see the social consequences of these qualities. However, plantains have a major drawback—they are poor in protein and other elements necessary for a balanced diet and must therefore be supplemented with other food. This quality leads to the "banana belly" seen on children who eat only plantains. This is not a problem among the Sebei, for they do grow other crops and have chickens, milk, and meat.

The Effect of War   The other set of events that affected the development of Sebei culture was warfare. We have already seen that the Bantu-speaking Gisu pushed the Sebei out of a sector of Mount Elgon. The Sebei successfully repulsed efforts by the Teso to make similar territorial inroads. But raiding by the cattle-keeping people to the north and east—the Karamojong, Pokot, Uasin-Gishu Maasai, and Nandi—was even more severe. Until supported by colonial protection, the plains north of the mountain had to be abandoned, except for occasional hunting trips. The raiding was so great that part of the mountainside was practically denuded of population, and the Sebei on the north slope welcomed into their midst their refugee kinsmen who had been pushed out of the western section by the Gisu.

Let us examine these events for their meaning to the cultural evolution of the Sebei. First was the environmental change that took place when the Sebei moved to Mount Elgon. Later, a change in technology occurred as the Sebei acquired two new crops that were particularly suited to this environment. The third factor was the pressure of warfare, which made it necessary to adjust their social institutions to the new conditions of life. These three external forces in the situation brought about a series of changes that altered the whole fabric of the Sebei social system.

2/The cultural heritage

What was Sebei life like when the Sebei arrived on Mount Elgon, carrying with them the millennia-old tradition of Nilotic pastoralism? This picture must be built out of several sources: the common features of the cultures shared by people who speak closely related languages, the description of what things were like in the past that have been handed down as a part of traditional lore, and the evidence in the continuing behavior of modern Sebei that manifestly harks back to olden times. We can be reasonably certain of the accuracy of this depiction, but must remember that it is a construction.

ECONOMIC ELEMENTS

The economy was a dual one. The men cared for the animals and the women milked the cows and cultivated small garden plots using iron hoes. We don't know which was of greater importance for food production, and it probably varied from place to place. But we can be certain that livestock was more important, socially and psychologically, because almost all the ritual activities centered on livestock and their products and not on gardens and agricultural products. Given the little rain and the low productivity of grains on the arid high plains from which the Sebei came, agriculture probably offered less food. Yet these farm products were essential to their livelihood, and all pastoral people require some access to them, whether through production or trade.

Animal Husbandry The demands made by the animals set the character and tone of life for people who focus their energy on livestock production. Animal husbandry requires special knowledge, hard work, and courage. The animals must be taken out to pasture each morning, they must be driven to water at least every other day, and they must be provided with salt. New pasture must be found each day. The animals must be kept together and, above all, they must be protected against predators, both animal and human. The men who herd the animals must at all times be prepared to face these dangers.

During the dry season the animals were kept away from the home area for months at a time, so that the young men, whose task it was to care for the

13

stock, lived in camps and led a bachelor's life together. Relatives brought them food from time to time, and young girls visited them for lovemaking (though this was not supposed to go any further than heavy petting, since uninitiated girls were expected to be virgins).

These young men began to learn animal husbandry by taking care of the sheep, goats, and small calves, herded together close to home. They learned the territory, where to find the grasses, what grass the animals prefer, how to spot new locations when an area was overgrazed, how to keep the animals from straying away, and how to keep a watchful eye for hyenas who are ever ready to pick off a lamb. One man told me that he learned this last lesson the hard way, receiving a severe beating when he brought back the flock of sheep with one missing.

Even earlier in childhood they learned the important lessons of animal husbandry in their play. Even today Sebei children still play at adult roles, using stones to represent animals.

We use the small stones for young cattle and the big ones for bulls; we find stones of special colors, and we give them the names of cows of that color. We exchange cows. If one of us wants to borrow a bull, he asks for it and pays a heifer for it, and then when the heifer has a calf we pay it back.

We also pretend that we are going to ask somebody for his daughter to marry, and then we pretend we go back after months and talk about payment. We use sticks to represent the cows and goats in counting what we will pay; we put down the bull for the uncle and then the sticks for the cows, and if we have no goats, we will add another cow, and so on. We pretend we have beer: once when we go to ask, once when we are counting out the sticks, and once when we come to get the daughter. We find a rock that represents the pot and we take long grass for beer straws. Then two of us will drag the girl home, telling her that her father has taken all the payment and that she shouldn't refuse, and we beat her with small sticks. When we get her home we have her cook food for our visitors and give her something to eat, but sometimes she refuses. We fear she will try to run away, and we watch her. We sometimes build a house so she will stay. We don't demand the "cows" back; we don't play to win or get anything.

We also play we take the cows to where they are kept in other men's *kraals*. Sometimes we slaughter them and sell them or pretend to eat them. We put the sticks down in a line and say we are circumcising boys; we pretend to be the fathers. We take a certain kind of grass and make a "knife" out of it and pretend to be cutting them. We also dance and pretend to slaughter a sheep and use mud for the smearing. Sometimes, one of them cries and we pretend to hold it down, and then we must bring a stone, for one has to pay a cow to the circumciser when one cries.

While boys and young men were herding animals belonging to their fathers, they were also beginning to accumulate some animals of their own. At about the age of eight, the two central lower incisors were removed, a practice that is ancient among these people. The Sebei say they do this so they will look like their cattle. A boy may have been given a sheep or goat—or even a calf— by his father or other relative for his show of bravery at such a time. Such an animal belonged to him, as did any kids or lambs or calves they produced. It was an important lesson in learning thrift and management, comparable to

Photo 3. Child playing with rocks as cattle. A kraal *is at the right.*

our paying children for chores or having them earn their own money so they learn how to manage it. Later, when the boy was initiated, more animals might be given him, if his family could afford to do so, so that by the time he was a bachelor in the cattle camp some of the animals would be his own.

Wealth Livestock among these people constituted their wealth, as well as being important to their sustenance. If a man was to be a successful Sebei, he had to build up his personal possession of livestock. The quickest way to do this was to take some from another person's herd. Raiding of this kind could escalate into warfare, and that is why keeping cattle was a hazardous activity and had to be placed in the hands of young men willing to engage in acts of derring-do. Of course, they had to be taken from enemies, people of other tribes. Since the cattle were branded (with cuts on their ears) and were individually known in the local area, they could not be taken from neighbors. Indeed, theft from fellow tribesmen was punishable, as well as morally reprehensible. But to go after cattle belonging to an enemy was honorable and risky.

It is debatable whether having wealth *confers* prestige or whether it merely *symbolizes* prestige, but in everyday life the distinction is not important. A man who had many cattle among the Sebei had prestige, whether it was because of the cattle themselves or whether it was because people believed that his having them showed that he had the qualities of courage, ability, and astuteness, they so much admire. Having wealth meant that he could get the things that are important, which among these people meant having wives and children and ultimately grandchildren, and which meant also having influence and leadership. So every ambitious young man tried to build up his herds to attain these social rewards and every young Sebei woman wanted a man with cattle so that she and her sons would prosper.

This was not merely pure competitiveness and individuality, though these qualities certainly existed. For success also required each person to collaborate with others to gain these ends: with his father and other family members when he was a child, with his age-mates when he was a young man, with his wives in producing and nurturing offspring, and with his lineage and clan when he was threatened with difficulty. Every society has institutions for such collaboration. The formalization of such collaboration is what we call the social structure or social organization. Let us look more closely at the Sebei organization as it existed in the beginning.

SOCIAL ORGANIZATION

Kin Groups First, each person was part of a family. The family was headed by the father, who may have several wives, each with her own children. These women each had a degree of independence, for each cultivated her own gardens, milked the cows allocated to her, and took care of her own children. Her sons were in a position to inherit the livestock (and their descendants) that had been given to her, or will be used by them to acquire wives. Each such family was part of a lineage called *kota* (*korik*, plural). The families belonging to a lineage were the descendants of a common ancestor, calculated patrilineally, that is, along the male line. The men of the lineage were expected to help and support one another in family disputes, bride payments, and many little ways.

These lineages were in turn each descended from a more remote common ancestor, also calculated through the fathers, to form a clan, called *aret* (*arosiek*, plural). These people were of one blood—the Sebei even believed they inherit certain traits, such as giving birth to twins or being hot tempered— and therefore men and women of the same clan could not marry or engage in sexual intercourse with one another. They also prayed and gave libations of beer to the spirits, *oyik*, (singular, *oynatet*), of their common clan ancestors. Most important of all, clansmen were expected to protect one another in major disputes. If a feud broke out between two such clans over a murder or the theft of cattle, all the members of the clan would have to stand together; if compensation for a murder must be paid, all men were expected to contribute cattle to the required *wergild*, as such payment is called. The spiritual unity of the clan ran deep in their belief, for if a rival group invoked an oath against anybody in the clan, the magic might strike death to any member.

Thus lineages and clans constituted major support groups; the lineages, made up of people who were closely related and usually living nearby, dealt with ordinary disputes of lesser importance; the clan, made of people more remotely related and often widely scattered, dealt with only the gravest issues, issues that were literally a matter of life and death. Lineages and clans did not own property, though the cattle were branded with clan marks, not individual marks, and in a spiritual sense, people seemed to have thought of them as a clan heritage.

To appreciate the importance of these collaborative units based on kinship, one must realize that the Sebei and their cattle-keeping kindred had no government, in the sense we ordinarily use that term. There were no chiefs, nor were there judges who could determine guilt and assess punishment. Clan leaders, who were normally the senior men of the senior lineages, had some authority within the clan, but it did not extend beyond the boundaries of the kin group. These were men, known for their wisdom and eloquence, who were brought in to hear disputes and help seek a solution, but they had no authority to render judgment (beyond their powers of persuasion) or punish offenders.

The Sebei and their neighbors did recognize the power of certain men as *prophets*. These men had access to the spiritual world and could foresee events, and their advice was sought before initiating any major undertaking, whether military aggression against an enemy or engaging in ceremonial activity. While these men were feared and respected (the Sebei use the same word for both these sentiments) and might be appealed to in case of disputes, they had no real authority. Indeed, prophets whose auguries proved wrong (or whose prophecies were unpopular) were sometimes killed. So in the absence of a formal government, the function of maintaining order was largely the responsibility of these essentially independent kin groups. Internally, order was maintained by the authority of clan elders. Between groups it was established by confrontation between two or more such groups. Normally, disputes were settled amicably, but they could lead to feud. Under such conditions, a strong bond between clansmen was clearly essential, and belonging to a strong and wealthy clan was an advantage.

Though in a legal sense each clan was independent, in another sense they were also interdependent. The rule against marriage between a man and woman of the same clan meant each person had to marry a person from another clan, a rule that is called *exogamy*. It follows from this that the clans were all interrelated through marriage. A person also had special responsibilities to the clan of his mother (and could also not marry a woman from that clan) and later would have special relationships to the clansmen of his wives and of the wives and husbands of his children. Thus each individual had a network of kin relationships that extended beyond his own clan, and these networks served to bind the people together—though this did not always prevent disputes from arising.

Each Sebei man normally wanted to have a number of wives and many children; real success for an old man lay in being the head of a lineage. Marriage in the traditional days of pastoralism was generally delayed until rather late for the men—perhaps over thirty—while women usually married soon after they underwent initiation. Children were seen as a source of immortality, for descendants gave libations to support deceased ancestors.

THE SOCIAL USES OF LIVESTOCK

Cattle and Marriage   Livestock played an important role in the organization of social relationships. A legal marriage required the payment of cattle; without the transfer of at least one cow, the children would be considered illegitimate. For a first wife, a man's father was expected to supply the animals, though other relatives were also expected to help. For subsequent marriages, the man himself usually supplied the animals. These marriage goods went to the family of the bride, the livestock mostly to her father though some were especially designated for the mother and the mother's brother. The bride payment in modern times includes many things beside cattle, and in the old days probably also involved beer, honey, small stock, and even everyday articles such as beer straws and mats. The amount varied according to circumstance, and nowadays it is closely and acrimoniously negotiated. (We saw earlier that the children played at such negotiation.) But some of the people closely related to the Sebei do not negotiate brideprice; rather, they transfer a standard amount or an obligatory gift that anthropologists call a *prestation*. So it may be that marriage among the Sebei did not always turn into the confrontation between the two families involved, as is the case in most of their negotiations today. These confrontations create a strain between the kindred of the marital pair. But whether the transfer of wealth to the bride's family was a standard payment or the result of close bargaining, in order to have wives and children a man had to have access to cattle.

We have seen that livestock were used as negotiable items in major disputes (*wergild*) and in domestic affairs (bride payments). We also saw animals

Photo 4. The "bull of the herd" belonging to Ndiwa arap Kambuya. The horns are artificially shaped.

used in other social negotiations as gifts, loans, or allocations, as for instance giving an animal to an initiate for bravery during circumcision. Some of these uses were of particular importance to social relationships, and we will mention two of them.

A man would allocate to each of his wives certain cows to milk. Some of these he gave to her, or "smeared," as the Sebei say, for it was a ceremonial act in which the cow was anointed. These cows became her property in the sense that she had the exclusive right to milk them, they were to be inherited exclusively by her own sons, and the husband could not dispose of them without her consent. These rules applied to all the offspring of such cows. The wife could not, however, dispose of them herself. Other cattle a man would keep exclusively to himself as *tokapsoi*, though the lactating cows among them would be turned over to a wife to milk.

Cattle Contracts   The second use of cows was in exchanges referred to as *namanya*. We saw that the children still incorporate this use into their play. This was an exchange of a bullock for a future cow. It was normally initiated by a man who wanted to slaughter an animal for a ceremonial purpose. He might seek out an exchange because he needed one of a particular color, but that was not necessarily the case, for it was considered good form to slaughter an exchange animal. For the bullock he received, he turned over a heifer to its owner, and this man would keep her until she had produced a female calf and that calf was ready to reproduce. At some time the original heifer (now of course a cow) was returned along with any male calves she may have produced, but her first female calf became the permanent property of the man who supplied the bullock. Today, such exchanges are still quite frequent among men who have much livestock; I talked to one who had over 30 such contracts involving cattle (nowadays, it can also be done with goats and sheep and even chickens and land) going at one time, some of which where he gave the heifer for a bullock and others in which he did the opposite. I found that over one animal in five in the census of cattle I took were animals either acquired as *namanya* or given out as *namanya*.

Since these contracts were fraught with all kinds of potential difficulties, since they created problems of keeping track without written records, and since they did not in fact increase the total available animals, it is reasonable to ask why the Sebei engaged in *namanya* negotiation. There were two reasons, which may really be different ways of expressing the same one.

First, they created a permanent bond between the two men engaged in the exchange. Henceforth they would address one another with a quasi-kinship term, "my *tilyet*," which may be translated as "my kin-of-the-cow." They were expected to be hospitable to one another, sharing beer and meat and possibly at one time even wives. Marriages between a son and daughter of men who are *tilyet* to one another were said to become happy marriages. In sociological terms, these exchanges extended the network of mutual obligation to persons who were neither age mates nor clansmen (though they could be either) and thus reinforced mutuality. "Sweet," according to a Sebei proverb, "is the kin of the cow." Another proverb says "*namanya* never rots," and I have seen men conclude a contract that had been initiated by their grandfathers. This is not to say that all men always lived up to their obligations. A wise Sebei had to be careful with whom he entered into such negotiations and might even surreptitiously try to monitor his *tilyet*'s *kraal*. And, as with debts everywhere, some had to be written off as uncollectible. Nevertheless, the net effect of the *namanya* exchange was to strengthen social ties.

The second reason was more practical. It was a technique for spreading one's risk, a kind of diversified portfolio for a people who really had only one kind of investment. Cattle constituted a form of wealth that is highly volatile; it was especially subject to sudden loss if disease hit a *kraal* or, what is more likely, a group of enemy youth attacked a *kraal* and disappeared with the animals in the dark of the night. When this happened, the owner suffered a loss but was not destitute, for he still had animals in other men's herds. Furthermore, if the attacked *kraal* contained cattle belonging to other men through exchange, these men would be more ready to undertake the hazardous task of trying to retrieve them.

There are some other points that should be made about the Sebei attitudes toward their livestock. Each man selected one bull that was large and had a fine spread of horns and perhaps a specially desirable color, which he called *kirkitaptoka*, the bull of the herd, whose movements he imitated in dance and to which he sang songs—a kind of embodiment of his personal ego. The history of the bull of the herd had to be known, for its dam should have been one that produced much milk and many calves. It could not have been one that was received in the bride payment, for one must not allow such an animal to service one's cows. Men kept such bulls until they became very old and then slaughtered them ceremonially and placed the skulls on the *kraal* gate.

AGE SETS AND INITIATION

Another institution established collaborative ties among Sebei men: *the age-set system.* Age sets are widely distributed throughtout East Africa and are, as already suggested, a functionally effective institution for the pattern of pastoral nomadism found there. An age set is a social unit that binds together the men who reached maturity at about the same time and underwent initiation together. The ritual bonds them into a permanent group with mutual obligations that continue through time until ultimately they all die off.

It is important to distinguish this idea, which is really not found outside East Africa, though there are comparable kinds of structures elsewhere, from *age grades.* Age sets are groups of men; age grades are sets of activities appropriate for men of a certain age. Thus as age sets are formed, the men together enter into the lowest rung of the age-grade system—junior warriors; as this group grows older, the age set graduates into the next age-grade level, senior warriors, and a new group of men with a different age set enters the age grade of junior warriors. As time passes, the surviving men move from grade to grade until they become old and die.

The Age-Set Cycle   The Sebei had a cycling system of age sets. There were eight such groups, each divided into three subsets. The eight groups were each named, the subsets formally labeled by their position in the sequence—first, middle, last—but also given a kind of nickname. The sequence was cycling, so that for instance, the Maina, who were initiated just before colonialism reached the area during the last decades of the nineteenth century, had previously been initiated about 160 years earlier, in the 1730s and 1740s. The Sebei think of this as a recurrence of the same period, as a kind of circular quality of time itself, but as they do not ruminate on these matters or express themselves clearly regarding them, I cannot say how precisely they perceived these metaphysical notions. They do refer to Maina times or Nyonki times and think that some are particularly fortunate or ill fated. These philosophical matters need not concern us, the more particularly because the Sebei are themselves very vague concerning them.

Each man joined his age set through initiation. We will later describe in greater detail this initiation as it is practiced today. It took place about every six years. The time was determined by the prophet on the basis of the maturation cycle of a vine found high on the mountain that flowers at intervals of five to seven years. This flowering was the cue to start the initiation of a new age set. The initiation started at the eastern edge, at Bukwa, and proceeded across the face of the mountain sequentially area by area until it reached

Bulegene. Thus, all the youths throughout Sebei who were initiated in the same year belonged to the same age set, but those who were actually initiated at the same place had a stronger bond, and a particularly strong bond existed between those who stood next to one another. The six-year bracket created a subset, and three consecutive ones, covering a period of about 20 years, constituted one of the named sets, such as Maina or Nyonki.

Initiation   The initiation itself was a series of rituals that extended over a period of as much as six months. It began with a ceremony of cutting and ended with rituals of release. Between the two rituals the initiates were secluded and under a set of taboos that had the effect of making them nonpersons. They also contested with one another and practiced the arts of warfare. In the final ceremony of release, they relearned the ordinary crafts of adult life and were ritually reintroduced to their mothers.

Girls underwent a counterpart initiation when they matured. The operation was a clitoridectomy and the removal of the labia minora. English-speaking Sebei also call it circumcision, and I will follow this practice. I do not know what the function of women's age sets was in the pastoral period of Sebei history; it has no function in modern Sebei life and, in fact, many women who had undergone circumcision could not even recall the name of their age sets. The ritual itself is, however, still zealously and almost without exception entered into by Sebei girls and has great importance, as we will see.

This *rite of passage* is a classic example of a ritual with the death and rebirth motif that is widely found in puberty ceremonies. As they entered the ritual, the boys and girls become nonpersons, not called by name but by a number, their restrictions and seclusion depriving them further of personhood, and their rebirth as new persons, with new names, meant that they were unknown and unknowing until the necessary rites were performed. There are many symbolic expressions of this deep-seated notion. The fact that this form of ritual is widespread and recurrent in tribal life suggests that it taps something deep in the human psyche, that it represents some kind of recurrent, perhaps universal truth about the nature of humankind. Unfortunately, however, the Sebei cannot offer us any further insight into this dark undercurrent of human behavior, and we must return to the more pragmatic aspects of this important ritual activity.

The mundane meanings of this most dramatic ritual are themselves very important. The ritual did two things: it transformed boys into men and it created a solid and permanent bond among men of common age that would subsequently prove most useful in their shared endeavors. Changing boys into men is no simple matter. It involves the transformation of public attitudes toward them and their attitudes toward themselves and their activities—what we call maturation.

Rites of passage are intended to transform attitudes. Consider our own rite of marriage, an event that shifts the bride's and groom's dependence and responsibility away from their parents and toward each other and the children they presumably will have. Attitudes toward them are supposed to change, for they are no longer in the marriage market and their attitudes similarly are expected to be different. This alteration of the public image is clear among the Sebei; they never refer to circumcised women as girls and to call a circumcised man a boy is a gross insult. We see some of the change in the face of an initiate beforehand, when he invited us to the rite, and later when he was undergoing it.

During the period of seclusion, the initiates were subjected to a program of hazing, indoctrination, and training. They were sent out to capture the

Photo 5. *A young man of Nyelit (the village next to Kapsirika) when he came to invite us to his circumcision. The pin on his shoulder was in celebration of Uganda's coming independence.*

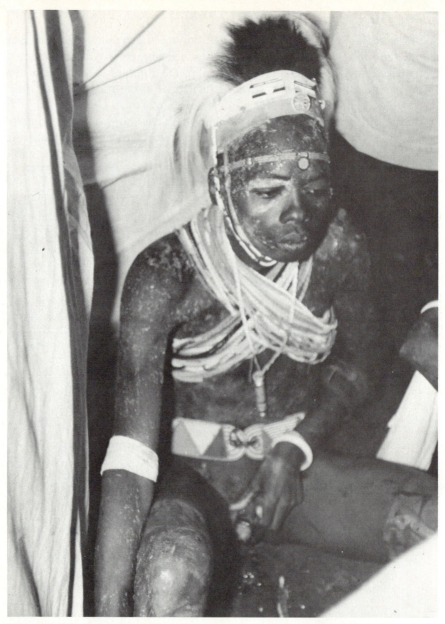

Photo 6. The same youth just after being circumcised. His belt was made by the Maasai; it was loaned by my wife and had to be redeemed with a gift, since he underwent the ordeal successfully.

lion in the dark of the night, only to learn that it was not real. They were made by their elders to perform impossible tasks and expected to obey such demands or face punishment. Anyone who has undergone a fraternity hazing or a marine bootcamp has some recognition of the effect such activity has on toughening attitudes and creating bonds among those who share these hardships and indignities. They learned secret lore involving, among other things, the control of magic (knowledge so esoteric that I was not allowed to learn it) and they underwent a constant barrage of moralizing by those already intiated.

All of these activities served both to transform the initiates into men and solidify these newly created men into a group that is strong and enduring. This group was expected to serve as a military unit to protect the animals and engage in the raiding that would increase the resources of the tribe, as well as add to their own possessions. There is no doubt in my mind that this is the primary purpose of the age-set system and the initiation. But traditional Sebei society and East African pastoral people in general attached greater importance to the system than merely serving a military function. Each age set occupied a kind of status: junior and senior military men, junior and senior elders. Age became a factor in public social relationships that found its expression in public debate, resolution of conflict, and even matters of protocol and manners. Thus, for instance, the men encircling a beer pot were ranged according to age, the senior men to the west. We must remember that age mates belong to different clans, so that the system served also to bind together men who were in a position of rivalry and potential hostility. In the absence of any governmental structure, these institutionalized interclan ties, together with the authority given to seniority, played an important integrative and decision-making function.

TERRITORIAL ORGANIZATION

Territory, or locality, is always one basis for social organization; people who live close together must recognize their own unity, even among people who are highly nomadic. At least two levels of spatial organization are found among the pastoral peoples of East Africa, and we may be sure that the Sebei had them as part of their system of social organization. The first of these is the tribe—or nation, as they are sometimes called, but it is a nation without political structure. The tribe is a community of people who recognize themselves as being related; they share a culture and a language, but their unity is more psychological than organizational.

The tribe is divided into smaller territories, in which, even without a political structure, active collaboration takes place. Usually such collaboration involves two things: a means of settling internal affairs by peaceable negotiations and a policy of mutual defense. We don't know what form of such territorial unity the Sebei had before they reached Mount Elgon, but in the next chapter we will see what happened when they established themselves on Mount Elgon.

Manyattas We do know that the Sebei used to live in large *manyattas*, for so I was told by old Sebei men and shown places where they had been. These *manyattas* were large circular areas enclosed by an impenetrable thornbush fence. As many as 40 households, or about 200 people, lived within the enclosure in a circle just inside the fence, while in the middle were *kraals* for the cattle of each herd. Adult men belonging to two age sets shared such a *kraal*, the men of each age set living in the same section. A central fire and a special place for holding discussions show that this was a true community. But these *manyattas* had been abandoned before any explorers reached the area, for they are never mentioned by early writers.

The *manyatta* structure is a kind of mobile village, for when necessary the whole community can change its location. These nomadic pastoralists had few possessions other than their weapons, clothing, and ornaments, except for the animals that could transport themselves. The houses were constructed of readily available materials—poles, grass, mud, and cow dung—with little labor.

Land We must realize that land among these pastoralists was seen as a public resource. Any man with cattle had access to any grass, water, and salt licks within the territory. It was sometimes said that God—*Asista*—made these elements for the cattle, and access to them was the inalienable right of the animals. When labor was invested in these resources, they became private property: when salt was taken back to the *kraal* from caves, that salt was owned; when a woman broke the sod with her hoe to cultivate a garden, that plot was hers so long as she continued to use it; when a man dug a well in a dry streambed to get water, he controlled access to that well—though he was expected to share it. These attitudes toward property were necessary to a sensible exploitation of semiarid lands, where animals are used to convert natural grass and brush into human food.

These attitudes toward land and place mean that locality was realtively unimportant as a dimension of social organization. We have already seen that there was no political structure; I think it was also true of the old Sebei culture that loyalties to and cooperation among people living in the same territory were never a prime factor in Sebei social life.

SUMMARY

Sebei social life was organized on three structural principles; the first was based on kinship, the units of family, lineage, and clan. Lineage and clan were essential legal entities. The second was based on age. Each man was initiated into a subdivision of an age set, and he retained a sense of belonging and loyalty to age set and the subset throughout his life. These units had a hierarchical order based on the principle of seniority. The third was territorial. There were probably three levels of territorial organization: the tribe as a whole, some local division of the tribe, and the residents of a *manyatta*, who actually lived in close collaboration.

In addition to these structural principles and in many ways cutting across them, was the ownership of livestock. Livestock constituted the Sebei wealth, and therefore the ownership of many animals meant high social standing. But livestock were also used in many different social transactions and therefore cemented alliances and created social bonds, thus making a fourth basis for social relationships.

3/The transformation
of Sebei society

When the Sebei brought their cattle and other animals up the slopes of Mount Elgon, they found a land that changed the relative effectiveness of their basic economic activities. What circumstances transformed their society into the kind of community it had become by the time the Europeans entered the area, in the closing years of the last century? Some understanding can be obtained through oral history and some is made evident by current practices. But we must put together the picture of these changes with informed guesswork. The Sebei do not tell us about their arrival; indeed, their myths assume that they are the descendants of *Masop*, as they call and anthropomorphize Mount Elgon. Whether it was inhabited by Cushitic people (as Benet architecture suggests) or Dorobo (who are usually found in mountain fastnesses in East Africa), we don't know. The mountain area varies, as we have already seen, and we may expect the progress to have been different in the west than it was in the east, as, indeed, are the current patterns of life.

SEDENTARIZATION

The very first thing to happen to the Sebei must have been a loss of nomadism; they settled down. The higher rainfall meant that the grass was more rapidly replenished and the permanent streams provided water for the stock near at hand. Salt, the third requirement of cattle, could be obtained as stone blocks broken from the walls of the many caves that perforate this volcanic mountain. Settled life led to more cultivation of gardens, which the greater levels of rainfall also made more productive. The humid regions in the west were poorly suited to cattle raising, and this made agriculture still more important. Later, when maize was introduced from what is now Kenya and when the cultivation of plantains was adopted from the Bantu peoples to the west, farming became the major productive enterprise, and in some areas the only means of getting a livelihood.

This new mountain habitat made the traditional patterns of cattle raiding more difficult. The steep escarpment formed a barrier to aggression from the outside and, at the same time, made raiding by the Sebei against neighboring territories more difficult. As we will see, the mountain was not as impregnable as the Sebei might have thought, and in later years the livestock, women, and children were often holed up in caves while the men fought off raiders. But the Sebei saw the cliffs and caves as an important refuge.

As farming increased in importance and cattle declined, families moved out of the *manyattas* and settled near the gardens they increasingly cultivated. Living nearby made it easier to work and harvest the crops and to protect them from birds, monkeys, and theft. The Sebei have always held that grazing land was public property, but that it transferred to private holding when work was expended on it. So as Sebei engaged in more and more farming, the amount of public land diminished and more and more was claimed by individuals. Nowadays, there are no public lands in most of the humid area of the west, but in the east, as well as on the plains and high up in the mountains, grasslands unsuited to cultivation are still available for livestock to graze, without delineated right to ownership.

Localized Communities This process of settling on the land being cultivated must have been initiated by individual men deciding one after another to leave the *manyatta* and settle on land they claimed as their own until finally the *manyatta* was entirely abandoned. This had profound effects on the character of the society. The first and most far-reaching effect was to make territorial social units more important. The whole of Sebei territory is now divided into units that can be delineated with lines drawn on a map. There are two classes of such units: the *sangta*, which I will call village, and the *pororyet*, which could be translated as parish or county, but as those are not entirely appropriate, I will call it by the Sebei word. The *sangta* has no center; it is not a cluster of houses and shops, as we usually imagine villages to be, but merely an arbitrary delineation of a small area that includes 20 to 40 individual households, spread more or less evenly over that area. Nor is there a center or focus for the *pororyet*, though there might be a sacred fig tree under which the men congregate to discuss matters of public importance.

The original meaning of the words *sangta* and *pororyet* tell us something about the transformation that took place. *Sangta* was the term for a place within the *manyatta* where the men gathered to discuss domestic affairs. Even down on the plains today, where a man may enclose the houses of his wives and his cattle byre with a brush fence, a place will be set aside for people to congregate to discuss family matters, and this is called the *sangta*. The *sangta* is now a congregation of domiciles, and its internal issues are essentially domestic matters.

The word *pororyet* originally meant battalion, the unit of military men under a single leader who fought together. It has been given a territorial meaning, but it retains some of its older implication. For when the Sebei still engaged in warfare, men of the *pororyet* fought together under a military leader. Furthermore, each *pororyet* had the right to decide on its own whether to enter into a combat to support actions initiated by or against another *pororyet*.

There is also a third level of spatial social division: the tribe. In the present territory of Sebei there were three such tribes, the Mbai, who occupy the most densely settled area in the west, the Sapiñ, who occupy the open areas of the east, and the Sor, who hold the transition area in between. There are small dialectal distinctions in the language of these groups, and I therefore think they represent an ancient territorial pattern. Indeed, they occasionally fought with one another in the nineteenth century, and some mutual hostility and expressions of prejudice remain. The unity of all Sebei tribes was expressed by the fact that they coordinated their rituals, which always started in the east and went successively westward, *pororyet* by *pororyet*. They also all recognized the same prophets. Today, while the *pororyet* and *sangta* retain some of their importance, the tribes do not.

THE ORGANIZATION OF WARFARE

Now this spread of the people over the land and the increased investment that the Sebei made in their real estate had significant consequences. For one thing, it altered the character of their warfare. The ancient pattern of raiding and counterraiding involved cattle; land was not at issue. Increasingly it began to involve territory, the defense of a homeland. Thus the battalion, the *pororyet*, which had once been a unit of military action, became the unit of mutual defense. Since the *pororyet* was the military unit, its membership had to be clearly defined—a people needs to know who their allies are and be sure of their loyalty. Each man belonged to the *pororyet* into which he was born. He might live in any *sangta* within the *pororyet*, and men not infrequently now have houses in two or more with a wife at each. But a man could not change his *pororyet* affiliation without a formal ceremony of departure and a formal ritual of acceptance. *Pororyet* affiliation was therefore fixed, and most traditional rituals were performed by the *pororyet* as a unit.

Changes in Warfare   The defense of a territory required the mobilization of all able-bodied men. Thus, warfare could no longer be treated as the province of the young; it was everybody's task. Warfare was no longer in the hands of the age set but of the *pororyet*, with the old men fighting along with the young. As one man told me, "The Sebei were not going out raiding but were defenders; you find brave people among the elders and the young men."

But if the military function was taken away from the age sets, as clearly the altered circumstances required, then the first and most important purpose of these units was lost. If the purpose was lost, then this organizational structure was not needed. Among the neighboring Nilotic people each age set has a structure of leadership that makes it an effective unit of action, but the Sebei did not recognize formal roles or offices within the age set. With the loss of both function and structure for the age sets, the whole system of age sets became weakened. While relative age is always an important consideration, authority no longer rested upon age sets as such. A man who was older should be shown deference and respect and is more apt to be listened to in councils but he had no formal authority. Age sets now have no political function whatsoever.

Let us be clear on what has happened here, because it is very important. Nowadays, each man continues to undergo initiation and emerges from it into the appropriate age set. He knows what set he belongs to and who among his acquaintances belong to his or another age set. One of the first things a Sebei tries to learn upon meeting strangers, as we like to know the occupation of a new acquaintance, is his age set affiliation. I was frequently asked what age set I belonged to, though nobody cared that I didn't belong to a clan. To his fellow age-set members, a man is expected to be polite and considerate and offer hospitality, to members of more senior groups he is deferential, and he expects deference from those who are his juniors. There is even some evidence that in modern political affairs, under the jurisdiction of the colonial and Uganda national government, political alignments are formed by men who are similar in age, but they are not expressed in terms of age sets. These matters have more to do with manners rather than with formal structure and social influence. In the last chapter we saw that the age sets, by uniting men from diverse clans offered a kind of authority system that served the interests of peace in the absence of any governmental authority, but for the Sebei this was lost.

THE CREATION OF COMMUNITY LAW

Traditional Law   With the Sebei living in increasingly crowded villages and the age-set structure having lost its function, there was a kind of power vacuum that needed to be filled. What happened is both interesting and significant. Some time around 1850, Matui, the most powerful prophet in remembered Sebei history, a man who lived in the most agricultural western section, began a new ritual and a new political institution that the Sebei call *chomi ntarastit*, which may be translated as passing the law. This was a ritual in which all the men swore that they would not break a set of specified rules, with the recognition that if one did, the other men of the *pororyet* had the right to punish him.

Before we describe this ritual, we must remember how legal cases had traditionally been settled. All important legal matters were considered confrontations between the clans of the two parties to the dispute. Let us say that a man of one clan, say Kapsombata, killed a man of another, say Kapchai, then all the men of Kapchai would seek revenge. There were three ways to settle the score. The first was to enter into a feud and try to kill a Kapsombata man—any man, preferably one of equal wealth and standing to their man who had been killed, and not necessarily the one who was the murderer. But the two clans might agree to a settlement, in which case the leaders would agree to proper compensation in cattle—perhaps a hundred head—furnished by the Kapsombata men and shared by the people of Kapchai.

Vengeance is chancy and settlement is difficult, so the men of Kapchai might follow a third alternative: placing a curse on the Kapsombata. There are diverse forms for oathing, but we may describe the kind that was done openly by the two clans, the kind that would be used if the Kapsombata denied that they had committed the murder. Members of the two clans, those who had suffered a loss and those accused, gathered by the path near the house of the accuser. A hole was dug, a number of posts from specified trees implanted in it and bound around with a poisonous liana, and the whole encircled with stones. This would be left in place so that people could see it "and know that something bad has taken place there." The accuser, the accused, men from their clans, and unrelated men gathered naked around this altar. They held their unsheathed spears against the base of the altar, or lunged at it, and swore as follows:

Accused: If I have killed your clansman, it will eat me.
All: Will eat you.
Accused: And if you libel me, it will eat you.
All: Will eat you.
Accuser: If I falsely accuse, it will eat me; if you have killed, it will eat you.
All: Will eat you.
Accuser: And if you have killed, it will eat you, and also your treasury [children and cattle].
All: Will eat you, my fellow; if you have killed, it will eat you; but if you have not killed, it will not eat you.

They sang a song at the end, thrust their spears at the base of the altar and then scattered in all directions.

Community Law   Matui took this oath and transformed it into an oath of allegiance. A similar altar was constructed, but to the magical plants already used he added, with appropriate symbolic significance, a plantain stem. All circumcised men of the *poroyet* gathered naked and swore as they thrust their spears at the altar: "If I kill a man, then this will eat me," and so with each of diverse crimes such as theft and arson. This oath was justification for the men of the *pororyet* to punish any man who broke it; that is, it was the recognition of the right of the community to assess guilt and punish the offender. The oath was intended to protect the weak, which is to say a man without local clansmen, against the strong; it was the first step in establishing community authority to find persons guilty and punish them for their acts. Clearly this was an effort to respond to the new situation created by the settling down of the population into permanent villages.

Chomi ntarastit was not very effective. For one thing, the punishment consisted of plundering all the man's stores of food and animals regardless of whether what he had done was a serious or a minor crime. Furthermore, it served as a strong deterrent only for a year or two after the oath was pledged. Matui should have ordered the ceremony each year or biennially, but instead he called up the ritual only after he found men disregarding it. These limitation, however, do not detract from the sociological significance of the innovation: circumstances changed creating a felt inequity and the community responded with a device that attempted to cope with it. This exemplifies the process of cultural evolution. It is also important to recognize that the device utilized the traditional institutions of oathing, not merely because it was traditional, but because attached to that oathing were the deep-seated sentiments and beliefs regarding supernatural forces.

CHANGES IN THE DOMESTIC SCENE

We turn next to another set of social consequences of the settlement of the Sebei on the land and their dependence on agriculture: the effect on domestic life. Under pastoral conditions, men generally remained bachelors for many years and then married as many wives as they could afford. Men's activities were largely separate from those of the women and the marital bond did not entail close daily husband-wife relationships. The man shared his meals and had sexual intercourse with wives in turn, except when they were menstruating or well into pregnancy and for a period after the birth of a child. Co-wives might have strong and friendly relationships and work together, which was the ideal, or might be jealous of one another and seek magical means of controlling their husband. But each woman had her own house, her own cattle, and her own children, and the bond between a mother and her sons was usually a close one. Each also had her own plot of land, but there was no scarcity of land. In fact, without fertilization and crop rotation, land became infertile after two or three years and a new plot had to be opened.

Land as Property But as agriculture took on major importance and especially as land cultivated to plantains became permanently useful, that situation changed. When families took up land, it was the men who claimed ownership, and they tried to treat land as they did cattle. That is, each man allocated some of the land to each of his wives for her to cultivate and held back some for his own use. The land allocated to each wife also was supposed to be shared with her sons when they married. In short, a pattern of behavior and attitudes suitable to the handling of livestock as property was transferred to land as property—and this created many difficulties.

First, while cattle are both the property and the responsibility of the men, land was the property of the men but worked by the women. Second, cattle increase in numbers by natural reproduction, but the land held is set and does not increase itself. Third, the land given to the son is taken away from land necessary to feed the wife, her other children, and her husband. Finally, because land is supposed to be turned over by a woman to the wife of her son, this inevitably further strained the relationship between a woman and her daughter-in-law—a relationship that is apt to be fraught with tension and jealousy even without such an extra burden. The system began when there was still much land and relatively few people, and under these circumstances it probably worked well enough. The decimation of the population by bloody wars probably enabled the system to continue for a long time. But by the time of my research, the strains and difficulties of this situation were quite apparent, as we will see later.

Among pastoral people, there are wide differences in the number of animals owned; some people are richer and some poorer. Certainly, also, a youth with cattle-rich parents has an advantage, just as the children of the wealthy are everywhere advantaged. But livestock constitute the kind of wealth that can be built up from scratch and, contariwise, can be lost as a result of a single raid or devastating disease. We sometimes speak of it as being a volatile kind of property, since it makes people subject to rapid changes in status. Stock people everywhere in Africa seem to recognize this and the distinction between rich and poor does not lead to social classes. A rich man's son would not be assured of wealth; a poor man's might rapidly rise. But when property was in land, which is not volatile, and especially as there was no more public land on which to settle, the distinction between rich and poor became more permanent. As we will see later, a sense of social class was beginning to develop in the parts of Sebei where landholding was most important.

We should stop to think about this change for two reasons; first, because it illustrates the process and second, because it can keep us from making the false assumption that what happened was inevitable. We saw that the shift from pastoralism to farming made it necessary for the Sebei to deal with the issue of control of land, which had become their principal resource. It was inevitable that some new rules had to be formed, but not necessarily the ones that emerged, and, in fact, matters almost took a different turn. The Sebei came close to adopting a pattern of clan control of land, which is frequently a solution among horticultural people. This would mean that each clan owned a block of land that was administered by the clan elders, who allocated portions to each clan member, according to need. There is evidence to suggest that the clans were more important in that part of Sebei territory that had been taken from them by the Gisu, who, it will be remembered, pushed the Sebei out of the western slope of Mount Elgon. For one thing, the wars that the Sebei fought were engaged in by clans—not by the *pororyets* as elsewhere. This suggests that these clans were territorial, though we do not know how they allocated land use. Aloni Muzungyu, the appointed chief of the Sebei during my first two visits, told me that he could never find out whether in the olden days land was owned by clans or by individuals, and I think this was because of this regional difference.

When the Sebei were driven out of this territory, they fled eastward and settled among the Sebei already living on the north slope. They settled as clan units, forming clan villages. Even today some villages are called by clan names, though by now only perhaps half of the residents belong to that clan. When they settled in this way, the clan elders must have allocated the land among the men. They tried to control access to the land by controlling to whom the land could be sold. But this attitude of communal control by clansmen came into conflict with another deep-seated set of traditional attitudes: individualism and the idea of the private ownership as it applied to livestock. While a clan council could prohibit a man from selling land that had been allocated to him to a person who was disliked—who, for instance, was suspected of being a witch—they could not prevent the man from selling it to an outsider. The idea of private right to land prevailed over the idea of clan rights; Sebei habits of independent ownership were too strong to permit clan control. They took the whole institutional apparatus of livestock ownership and control and applied it to land ownership and control. It was, as we will see later, a pattern not particularly well-suited to the new situation.

In the evolutionary process, the past tends to live on in the present, and established habits of mind may prevail and inhibit the development of more effective institutions. Ecological adaptation reshapes institutions to meet new circumstances, but it does not create perfect solutions.

THE CHANGING PATTERN OF SEBEI CAREERS

The transformation in the centuries between the Sebei invasion of Mount Elgon and the coming of Europeans involved both obvious and subtle shifts in life-style. The two models of economy—pastoralism and farming—are about as different from one another as any found among tribal societies. They make very different demands on the people and require different kinds of social relationship. To me, the key to this difference is in the way the individual *career* is formed. The traditional expectations of Sebei men had been to build herds and with them to acquire wives and children, a career full of challenges and difficulties but one that gave great satisfaction to a person with the right attitudes, knowledge, and will. The behavior that led to success for Sebei men living a horticultural life was not so clearly defined. Success was more dependent upon the agricultural productivity of the women and the ability to control land—and this was often a matter of how much land his father had established rights to.

It is more difficult to characterize what the change meant for women, whose careers also were altered. They had to work harder than their pastoral sisters, but they had more association with other women and perhaps more informal domestic authority. They more rarely had to share their husbands with other women, but when they did it was probably fraught with more conflict, since a finite amount of land had to be shared with the new wife. We will look at these domestic matters more closely later in the book.

THE COMING OF EXTERNAL CONTROL

The Sebei were undergoing the turmoil of these transitions when a new set of events changed their lives even more profoundly: the advent of colonialism. The first intimation of change came before a white man set foot on the mountain in the form of Swahili trade caravans. There was no slave trading, though the Sebei remember in song that one of their girls went off with a Swahili trader. From them they bought their first cotton cloth. The first European to go to Sebei and write about it appeared in 1890 and, in 1898 Sebei territory was used as a supply base for the Juba expedition and

Photo 7. A Sebei warrior in 1890. The photo was taken by Gedge, a member of the first party known to have visited Sebei. The shield is made of buffalo hide.

the Nubian "rebellion." Herbert H. Austin, who was in charge of this expedition, describes the people as follows:

> The natives in many respects are not unlike the Wa-Kikuyu [a people of Kenya], as they smear their bodies over with the same chocolate-colored clay, liberally mixed with fat, and work their hair into the similar mop-head style. Their ears are, however, not distended to quite so great an extent, and they wear few ornaments beyond a little iron chain and iron wire round their necks and wrists, and perhaps an ivory bracelet in addition round their biceps, whilst a leather belt, adorned with cowrie shells round the waist, is also very generally worn by the young bloods. A small goat-skin, well cured and greased, and soft as chamois leather, is thrown jauntily over one shoulder, whilst in his hand the young warrior carries either a long-handled spear with a small blade or bow and arrows, and a long, narrow, oval-shaped shield of thick hide.
> The elder women wear two hides, and are satisfied with a ring or two of iron wire round the neck, and similar ornaments round the wrists. They are great smokers, and, like the elderly ladies of Kavirondo, strut about with pipes, consisting of small earthenware bowls, to which are attached long wooden stems.
> The young unmarried girls wear a very simple costume, consisting of a ring or two of iron wire round the neck and a small leather apron 8 to 9 inches square, or a fringe of beads, not unlike rosaries, of the same size, which depends in front from a girdle round the waist, whilst a similar, though somewhat larger, covering of hide falls behind.

Though a few skirmishes and some deaths resulted from the tensions of that yearlong occupation, the chief difficulty came from the large amount of food traded in exchange for beads and other goods. This so depleted their food supply that the Sebei suffered much from the subsequent famine and the outbreak of rinderpest. They were in no condition to withstand the next onslaught. By then the British were in firm control of the great kingdom of Buganda on the north shore of Lake Victoria, which is now the hub of Uganda. With the British carefully looking the other way, an ambitious military leader from Buganda named Semai Kakunguru led an expedition to "tame" the wild tribes of Bukedi, the Baganda's word meaning "land of the naked people"—that is, savages. The conquest of the Sebei was one of Kakunguru's exploits and his men were set up as local overlords. They initiated a harsh rule (remembered with great bitterness when I arrived nearly 50 years later) that was somewhat mitigated 10 years later when British colonial personnel, with less harsh and more paternalistic attitudes, took control.

The establishment of external rule stopped the natural progress of transition from pastoralism to farming. It established new rules and regulations by fiat, as well as new opportunities and involvements. Among the many changes was the elimination of the prophets, who were seen as subversive. This deprived the Sebei of their one cohesive institution and led to the abandonment of most of their sacred and unifying rites. They established a court system made of a peculiar melange of Baganda, British, and Sebei practices. This took away an important function of Sebei clans and substituted witnesses of questionable veracity for the use of sacred oaths. They also established a governmental bureaucracy with a hierarchy of officials and elementary schooling for children.

A Western economy with markets and money led to increased dependence on purchased goods and production for export, the most important of which was coffee. The contemporary situation, to which we turn next, was affected by these later changes as well as the earlier ones.

4 / Sasur: The farming community

THE RESEARCH PROGRAM

In the preceding chapters I have outlined a broad view of Sebei institutions and the changes over time, giving us the organizational context of Sebei life. Now we will look at their daily life. In this chapter we will examine the village of Sasur near Sipi in the densely settled farming sector. In the next chapter we will look at Kapsirika on the plains below the mountain, where herds of livestock are kept much as they were in the old pastoral days. Though we will concentrate our attention on Sasur, we won't limit ourselves to events that took place in that village, but must draw on other experiences from the Sipi region. I will describe the events in the present tense, the "ethnographic present," but they apply to the way the Sebei lived when we were there in 1954 and 1961–1962.

Preliminary Study   First I will describe our research program. When I first visited the Sebei, I was on a Fulbright Fellowship for the year 1953–1954. In those days that program was very freewheeling; its purpose was more to create a group of scholars with competence in foreign areas than to produce specific research results. The United States discovered in World War II that our nation had too parochial an outlook, and Senator Fulbright saw the need to create a more international perspective. I thus went to Uganda with no plan other than to engage in ethnographic research in Uganda among a people whose culture had not been adequately recorded.

With the advice of the late Sir Andrew Cohen, then the governor of Uganda, I selected the Sebei, about whom there had been written only a few chapters by the anthropologist-missionary John Roscoe, who had made a brief visit to Mount Elgon in the early 1920s. With my wife, Gale, and my son, Mark (then seven years old and also on a sabbatical from his school), we climbed the escarpment and established our residence in an abandoned mud and wattle house in the *sangta* of Binyinyi. We spent six months doing research, mostly on traditions and history.

The Culture and Ecology Project   I also saw that there were great regional differences among the Sebei. These differences were not merely economic, but involved the character of social relationships and personal outlook. I decided that I would have to study these variations in order to come to a

39

satisfactory understanding of their culture. Furthermore, as mentioned in the Preface, I thought that these differences could demonstrate the process of ecological adaptation. Therefore, in collaboration with four other anthropologists and a geographer, I organized an expedition in 1961 involving the study of four tribes, each of which had undergone similar transformations.

The thesis that informed this research involved the recognition that, within the broad context of East African indigenous cultures, environment was the independent variable, that institutions (the dependent variable) altered as a result of an adaptive process, and that this process involved individual choices of action that constituted the intermediate variable. An ethnographer was responsible for the general study of each tribe (myself with the aid of my wife, for the Sebei). A geographer, Philip W. Porter, studied the environment and land use patterns for all the tribes, and a psychological anthropologist, Robert B. Edgerton, studied the attitudes, sentiments, and perceptions of individuals.

We wanted to make detailed investigations of two communities within each tribe, one community that represented the region devoted to more intensive agriculture, the other an area of more pastoral pursuits. For the Sebei, the *sangta* of Sasur represented the farmers and the *sangta* of Kapsirika the pastoralists. We divided our time between the two communities, establishing a household in each and living in them alternately. We used the villages as statistical bases for a series of questionnaires about demography, livestock ownership and use, agriculture, and other matters. These villages also constituted the sample for the psychological tests conducted by Edgerton and the more detailed aspects of the geographical investigations made by Porter. Of course, our ethnological investigations were not limited to these two villages, but these were the neighbors we got to know best.

Sasur is in the Sipi region, the center of the old Mbai tribal territory and an area of intensive plantain cultivation. We wanted to live in the village, but in order to do so we had to have a house. We negotiated with Maunya arap Salimu, whose land lay close to the road, to let us build a house on his property. For the privilege, he would have the house after we left.

The house was built in the native manner, but much larger, about 25 feet in diameter. After the ground was cleared, posts were set in a circle, about four inches apart. Stringers connected these posts to a center post. A door frame and three window frames, with solid wooden door and windows, were bought in Mbale and set in by a specialist. When the frame was finished, the roof was thatched. Then mud was plastered in the walls and the floor covered with mud and pounded. Because we were paying two shillings (28 cents) for each load of grass or poles, we had an abundant supply, so that the house was exceptionally well made. A smaller house served for our help, and a latrine was dug deep into the ground in the shade of the nearby plantain *shamba*. All the negotiation and building took us over two months. But in the end we had a snug and comfortable house that never leaked a drop of rain throughout the year in which well over 100 inches fell on it. It had two drawbacks. It was sited in a place where groundwater seeped, and so the floor was always damp and we had to learn to put our feet directly into our boots, and it was so dark that even in the daytime it was necessary to work by the light of kerosene pressure lamps—a disadvantage greater to an anthropologist than to a Sebei.

Photo 8. Our house in Sasur.

HOUSEHOLD AND HOUSEHOLD TASKS

Sasur is bisected by the road that runs across the escarpment. The Anglican primary school is there and it is but two miles to the town of Sipi, which had shops, a beer parlor, and the subdistrict headquarters. The Catholic mission school and dispensary are also nearby. Sasur consists of 77 households with a total population of 400 scattered over four-tenths of a square mile: a density of 1000 persons per square mile. About 75 percent of the land is under cultivation. The major crops, in order of importance, are plantains, coffee, maize, yams, and millet. Each household also has a kitchen garden for fresh vegetables. The fields, for which the Sebei use the Swahili word *shamba*, vary in size from two-tenths of an acre to over 2 acres, but are generally about a quarter or half acre. The typical woman cultivates about six such *shambas*; older women generally have more and younger women fewer, reflecting the growing pressure on the land. In 10 of the 60 households sampled, the men are polygynous, with two wives in eight instances and three in the other two cases. Two households consist of unmarried men. Each wife in the polygynous households has her own house and cultivates her own *shambas*.

Women are the hub of all work activity. They do all the household chores that they cannot put on their daughters, they care for the infants, carrying them in slings on their backs when they go to cultivate their *shambas*, and they haul wood up the mountainside on their backs and five-gallon tins of water from the stream on their heads. Young girls are expected to help in these tasks from about the age of five on. Older sisters often sling infants on their backs as they go playing with other children. If there are no older

Photo 9. Sebei women near Binyinyi peeling plantains and gossiping. The girls standing are inviting them to their initiation; the old woman has made an unpleasant remark that has angered the woman in the background.

sisters, a niece or other relative will be brought in to aid in these domestic chores, to serve as *mwet* (*mwenik*, pl.), as they call such child-helpers.

The men take full responsibility for cultivating the coffee, though women might help in harvesting the beans and in the arduous task of drying and pulping them. Where possible, the men also work for cash as governmental

Photo 10. A mwet *(child nurse) carrying her young sibling.*

employees. A few have cattle that, except for the occasional cow needed for milk, are kept on the plains under contractual arrangements with men there. These men may be relatives, but the contract can be made with any man the owner trusts. Men are not very busy.

The Moyket   For the ordinary tasks of gardening, a woman works alone or with a friend or co-wife, but when the task is large, such as cultivating a *shamba*, she will organize a work party, or *moyket*, to get the collaboration of many. She must first prepare native beer of maize or plantains. This takes many days of work. First she grinds the corn (or takes it to the mill to be ground). She mixes the meal with water and lays the mash down in a pit dug under the eaves of the house. She must line the pit with plantain leaves and carefully fold them over the mash before she covers it with earth. It ferments for about two weeks. She then takes the mash out and fries it on a large metal sheet over an open fire. She softens it with water and mixes in sprouted millet that acts as a malting agent. She puts this mixture in large pots of water that are stored in a warm house—preferably that of an old woman who likes to keep her home warm—where it ferments one or two days.

On the day the beer is ready the women gather to work; men also sometimes participate. Each works throughout the morning and stops at about two in the afternoon to go home to clean up before joining the beer party. The hostess serves beer in the large pots in which it has been fermenting, each guest brings her own straw made from a liana, which may be as much as eight feet long. The workers sit around the pots enjoying the beer and the social occasion until nightfall.

The *moyket* socializes women's labor. Since every woman is alternately both host and guest, it does not save labor, it merely renders work less irksome. No one sends invitations; people learn of the work party and come or not, as they wish. Of course, a woman who does not help others may not have helpers in return. Since 20 or 30 persons participate and since each woman has several *moykets* a year, such beer parties are a regular and recurrent aspect of Sebei social life.

Such activity is seen by anthropologists as reciprocity, and the Sebei think of it in these terms: you do for me and I will do for you. But everybody also has a clear idea of what is expected, and expresses displeasure if it is not met. I collected data on ten *moykets* in Sebei that show that these social calculations have an economic side. I found that the average cost of the beer furnished to the 295 workers in these *moykets* was 2.08 shillings (1 shilling equals 14 cents). This figure is close to the two shillings that one would pay for an afternoon around the pot at a Sebei-run beer parlor. It is also the prevailing minimum daily wage for common labor. The figures varied around this average, but the person who gave the least beer had received many complaints while the one who offered the most had received much praise. Six people indicated that they provided separate pots for the men and women workers, and the average value for the men was 2.52 shillings, for the women was 1.86 shillings. That seems very much like the gender discrimination familiar to us.

Photo 11. A moyket *in Sasur. Plantains in the background. The hoe blades are purchased, but the handles are made by the Sebei. The heavy African sod requires the thrust of the short-handled hoe.*

Photo 12a. Sebei drinking beer around a pot with their long beer straws.

Nonworkers also enjoy the beer. In those 10 *moykets* analyzed, 30 guests had been invited, 16 of whom were relatives, 5 were *tilyet* (kin of the cow), 5 were age mates, and 4 were friends. Matters get more complicated. A man may come by to beg beer and be offered a tube; he will then sit on the edge of his chair and suck until others around the pot complain. Men come to sell roasted bits of meat or cigarettes and are similarly invited to have some beer. The host may hold some beer back for a party that night or have a pot for sale (thus discouraging beggars).

My neighbor Lasto held a *moyket* employing eight men and eight women for cultivation and four men for pruning coffee. Around the workers' pot were six others. They were: (1) a man who helped pour the beer; (2) a man who was circumcised right next to Lasto, so that Lasto said, "He has my blood on his body, he cannot pay for beer in my house"; (3) a man of Lasto's age set invited for no special reason; (4) the man who furnished the special plantain leaves used to line the hole in which the mash is buried while it ferments; (5) an elderly neighbor and classificatory mother's brother invited because "our wives are of his clan"; and (6) a man who, seeing it was about to rain, built a shelter of poles and banana fronds to protect the drinkers, and therefore was invited by the workers.

Inside the house was a noisier pot—perhaps because these guests had not worked and therefore were not so tired. Lasto identified them: his brother ("the one who will bury me"); a man with the same name as another

Photo 12b. *Sebei women drinking beer on a ceremonial occasion for which some have been garlanded with vines.*

brother ("his *oynatet*, soul, is the same as my brother's, and he would have had the brother's share if he had come first"); his father-in-law; the wife of his father's brother (who is like a mother and therefore has the mother's share), and his wife's mother's sister's son and daughter-in-law (with whom Lasto and his wife have a long-standing reciprocal beer-sharing relationship). Those who were not kin included two age mates and a special friend and their respective wives, an old woman of the neighborhood, a Pokot woman (out of kindness), a *tilyet*, a neighbor, and the quasi brother already noted.

Such special guests are said to enjoy certain "meats" of the beer pot. Here we have an example of the adaptation of an old cultural practice to a new social situation. When a man slaughters a bullock, usually for some ceremonial reason, specified cuts of the animal are destined to go to particular persons: the hump to a real brother, the heart and right thigh to clan brothers, the rump to the father-in-law, an area inside the hind legs to the father (for it is the part of the flesh from which the owner came), the ribs to the *tilyet* from whom the animal was obtained in *namanya* exchange, and so on. These meats have been transferred to the *moyket*, an appropriate extension of traditional hospitality to the new agricultural situation, where slaughtering is rarely possible, but beer is frequent.

LAND IN SASUR

Three old men live in Sasur whose fathers had settled there after they were forced out by the Gisu military pressure on the western slope of Mount Elgon. Each had inherited a large tract of land that the men, in turn, divided among their sons, whose own children were now growing to maturity. One of these three men is Lasto's father, Lewendi; another is Boror, who had been an important Sebei political figure but was now quite frail (he died while we were living among the Sebei), and the third is Psiwa.

Psiwa is a very shrewd old man. I spent a great deal of time with him, because he was always involved in something interesting; he served as ritual leader for various domestic rites, tried to settle disputes within the family, and was reported to have control of a kind of witchcraft, though of this I have only indirect knowledge. Psiwa had been busy building up his estate for the six mature sons that his two wives had produced and for his grandchildren. Philip Porter and I tried to map the holdings of the entire family but there was too much land in so many small parcels that we never finished; yet we learned a great deal about land ownership, land practices, and land disputes in the process.

The first people pushed out of the west by the Gisu were said to have merely expropriated land in Sasur, sometimes even driving off others. But the later ones, like Psiwa's father, had to purchase land, giving a bull or some goats. As late as 1927, a *shamba* was bought for five *warek* (the Sebei word for sheep and goats together). But soon thereafter, money was required for land purchases. Cash became increasingly important with the introduction of coffee. In the 1950s the average price was 750 shillings ($104) per acre, according to an analysis we made of 17 measured plots that had been sold for cash. Out of 246 Sasur *shambas* on which I have data, 70 percent were inherited from the father, 21 percent had been purchased, and 9 percent were borrowed under a *namanya*-like or other contractual relationship.

Men sell their land for various reasons. In three instances, the seller needed money to pay a son's brideprice; two needed money to pay indemnities resulting from a court case; three cited various other crises (school fees, wife's illness); two sellers were leaving the area; and another, who had acquired the *shamba* in compensation for the killing of his cow, found that it was too far from his home. The motivation for purchase were not often expressed, but one buyer wanted to have land in a separate place for his second wife, as the two women were quarreling too much, and in two other instances purchases were made in anticipation of taking a second wife. Land is not a part of brideprice, but if a man has land and no cattle he may sell some land, and occasionally the bride's people will take land in lieu of cattle.

Bargaining for Land   Let us sit in on part of the bargaining over land that Andyema, one of Psiwa's sons, was purchasing from a man name Musani, who already had used that *shamba* as collateral for the loan of 250 shillings. He now needed more money to pay his taxes. It was three-tenths of an acre of good but steeply sloping land with a large rock outcrop at the top. Musani and his friend, Seswet, as well as Psiwa, Andyema, three others of Psiwa's sons, a neighbor named Ndiwa, and the local chief were present.

When we arrived, Musani said that some newly planted plantains on the north border were an encroachment onto the land, and the men all began to search for the *senchontet* plants that are used to mark the border between holdings. Young *senchontet* plants were found that had altered the boundary and all agreed where the real boundary had been. Musani marked off the old boundary by cutting the bush and setting stakes. The neighbor who had encroached on the land later claimed that the piece had been given to him by Musani's father. Bargaining proceeded on the assumption that the whole piece was involved, without reference to this potential impairment. The land was paced off by Ndiwa, as a neutral party, while everybody watched carefully and representatives of both sides noted down the figures. Musani said that the land included the large rock, but Psiwa pointed out that this was not land that one could cultivate and rejected its usefulness for a residence site, saying, "That is part of the land that you can keep."

The men gathered at the upper boundary, Musani and his friend Seswet stood up on the rock; Psiwa sat hunched up to one side below them, while Andyema (the purchaser) stood farther below them with his brothers; Ndiwa and the chief were behind them. After some banter (including the suggestion that if there were arguments later they could write to me in the United States), they said there should be two sides with three men on each.[1] I declined an invitation to serve, so the seller asked Seswet and my interpreter, Chemtai.

Somebody said that the seller should first name his price, and Musani indicated 1000 shillings. Ndiwa countered with 300 shillings. Seswet was asked to speak next but he deferred to Chemtai who said 600 shillings. The chief took time looking over the land; he finally announced 350 shillings as the right price.

Seswet(s):   I am always attending bride bargaining, and they always give examples and that is why I'm going to tell you what I will say: you should realize that this will be your land for good, but that the money will be spent and finished. The people will agree with me, and I will say that the land should cost 750 shillings. I have sold many *shambas*, and I know how to bargain the prices.

Andyema(b):   I will give 450 shillings.

Musani(s):   Please pay me the 750 shillings.

Andyema(b):   Give me an example before charging me like that. Also, this land has banana weevils on it.

Seswet(s):   I sold my own land of 21 by 43 paces and got 650 shillings.

Andyema(b):   You got that price because many people were buying.

Seswet(s):   Also another piece of land, 31 by 71, that cost 650 shillings.

Andyema(b):   I insist on 450 shillings.

---

[1] In the discourse that follows, I will mark the men on the seller's side with (*s*), those on the buyer's side with (*b*).

Musani(s):   I insist on 600 shillings. You will keep the land forever.

Ndiwa(b):   If you agree, make it 500 shillings.

Musani(s):   No. One can get a cow for 500 shillings and eat the meat and it is finished; yet this land is permanent.

Sirar(b):   Prices for cows have now dropped. Lazima bought land from Andyema for 500 shillings.

Musani(s):   I paid 500 shillings for a piece 9 by 21.

Seswet(s):   We won't ask for all the money right away; we will take pay in installments.

Andyema(b):   I agree to 500 shillings.

At this temporary impasse, a number of side remarks were made; Andyema spoke of the lasting friendship that the sale would create between them (apparently in analogy to the *tilyet*). Lazima, one of the brothers, suggested that if Musani did not like the price he could seek another buyer.

Seswet(s):   Lazima is ruining the conversation by telling his brother not to buy the land! He is not happy to see his brother get the land. You must realize that Musani has dropped from 1000 to 600 shillings.

Psiwa(b):   How many cows would you have to sell to get 1000 shillings? It is mere bush. You should accept 500. You can buy three head of cattle for that. It's enough to buy a wife.

Musani(s):   I already have taken 250 from you [on a loan, using this land as security]. Are you going to give me only 250 more?

Psiwa(b):   I agree my son should give 500 shillings. He will have to sell something to raise the money. Don't take too much argument on this bush. If there was to be a *moyket* on the land, it would only take 10 people to do the cultivation. Some of this land is covered with rocks.

The bargaining continued, with buyer and seller reluctantly inching toward one another between 550 and 600 shillings. The conversation occasionally moved away from the bargaining to relieve tension. It continued:

Musani(s):   OK, at 550 shillings if cash, but not in installments.

Chemtai(s):   You should agree to 580; he is giving you a long time to pay.

Psiwa(b):   It is still a debt to be paid.

Seswet(s):   Bartega bought land at 100 shillings and sold it at 1000; don't you remember that?

Andyema(b):   Perhaps we will give you a bull to cover this amount.

Seswet(s):   How big a bull to cover such an amount? Pay the 580 shillings. You will have no quarrel with any of your wives, for they will have land to cultivate.

Andyema(b):   After paying you, the chiefs will arrest me for not having money for paying my poll tax.

Seswet(s):   Psiwa knows where to get money for your poll tax.

Psiwa(b):   No, I've already sent him away [i.e., given him his inheritance;

though he had not, as everybody must have known]. He has his own property.

Sirar(b): It is a very small piece of land.

Seswet(s): Do you mean to say that a man who is very small can't serve his wife right? I never heard of bargaining over a wife where they belittled the daughter as you are belittling our land here.

Musani(s): The money I get will be divided so many way there will be nothing left; I'm giving 20 shillings to you. [The bargainers receive a small compensation.] Give me the 580. My people have asked 600, and I have broken them by charging only 580. I've been too lenient.

Lazima(b): If our people insist on the 350 shillings that they started with, what would you say? But the buyer has been anxious to buy and has raised to 550. If it weren't for that rock, we would agree to a higher amount.

Musani(s): I know you, Lazima; you always want to buy at a cheaper price. If you were selling, the price would be 1300 shillings.

Psiwa(b): In the old days, this would have only cost one he-goat.

Seswet(s): In the old days one could borrow land for three years without paying anything and could sell the millet for a cow and become rich.

The contract was concluded at 560 shillings. While the substance of the bargaining is like haggling everywhere, the comments and analogies are peculiarly Sebei. The constant reference to livestock and the analogies to wife purchase hark back to tradition.

Land Disputes In our efforts to map Psiwa's land, we uncovered ten boundary disputes. Seven of these were internal to the family, two of which were disputes between co-wives of Psiwa's sons, three between Psiwa and his sons, and two between brothers. Three of the disputes were with neighbors, one with his contemporary, Boror, another with Boror's clansmen, and the third was a dispute of the kind that took place on the piece we saw being purchased, which had occurred before Psiwa bought the land.

We witnessed a major confrontation of the cases between two co-wives. They were widows of a deceased son of Psiwa, who had received the land from Psiwa when he married his first wife and then divided it between the two women when he married the second. The two women had been inherited by different brothers. Yapyego, the younger wife, proceeded to uproot the *senchontet* and cultivate the whole plot, right in front of everyone. Yapyego claimed to be more *poswama*, harder working, and more productive, and felt that Salimu should have divorced his first wife and also denigrated her for having but one son. Yapyego's present husband tried to stop her, but she paid no attention. Ultimately, the matter was decided in a kind of family court before Psiwa, some of the witnesses to the original allocation, and the local chief. The *senchontet* was replaced.

One of the conflicts between Psiwa and his sons was over their complaint that he was taking away land that was due to come to them when the old man died. They claimed Psiwa had reallocated land between his co-wives.

Psiwa denied this; he insisted that it was actually land that had not been given to either wife, but kept in reserve for himself. He also said that he had given each of his sons their land, except for the youngest, who would inherit the remainder of his mother's land. Furthermore, he was concerned about the adequacy of land for the still junior sons by his second wife. The sons attacked Psiwa physically and he took a court case against them and each was fined 50 shillings.

Land is the crucial resource of the Sebei living in Sasur and the whole western part of the escarpment. This area was gradually crowded with people so that land became increasingly difficult to acquire. Men like Psiwa understand this and try to build up their holdings; others do not seem to appreciate its full value. Since my investigations led me to estimate that a man could earn 1000 shillings per year off of coffee land, the price of land seems quite low. (Though earlier the government subsidized the planting of coffee, there now are controls on the increase in coffee acreage because of international coffee quotas. Under these new regulations, a man theoretically could not extend his coffee planting but I believe some did so.) Since land is crucial, we should not be surprised that it is the focus of disputes. Some of these disputes, such as the one between Psiwa and his sons that led to violence, arise because the Sebei came to treat land as they do cattle. That is, they allocate land to their wives and keep some for themselves as *soi*, to use the Sebei term. We will examine in more detail the kind of difficulties this engendered later in the book. There is also the ever-present possibility of conflict between neighbors, conflicts over just where the boundaries lie, as we have already seen.

RITUAL ADAPTATION

Conflict between neighbors was so endemic among the agricultural Sebei that they transformed an old family ritual of amity, *misisi*, into a neighborhood gathering, *mukutanek*. Let us look at this, for it is an example of how institutions are subtly reshaped in the evolutionary process to meet new exigencies.

Misisi used to take place in October after the millet was harvested. The grain is plucked in the head, and the ears are set out on mats to dry in the sun and then put, still in the head, in granaries. Some grain falls off, and these gleanings, called *misisi*, are collected and used for making beer for the harvest rite that took its name from these gleanings. *Misisi* was a feast with food as well as beer, and a bullock if it could be afforded. Libations of beer were poured for the ancestral spirits by the host's father, who says, "By brewing this beer, we say that there had been darkness and now light is coming with the new crops." The good spirits are offered beer inside the house and are mentioned by name; they include the host's fathers, brother, mother, mother's brothers, grandparents, fathers-in-law, brothers-in-law, and all the deceased members of the host's clan whose names are known and who

Photo 13. Pouring a libation of beer from a gourd dipper at the entrance to the kraal.

have living descendants. A failure to mention an ancestor might annoy the spirit. Libations are poured for the evil spirits away from the house or *kraal*, using the left instead of the right hand. Evil spirits may also be mentioned by name and will include those relatives who have died without progeny and are therefore jealous, or those who cursed a kinsman when he was alive. They are thus placated but kept at a distance.

As with Thanksgiving feasts among us, the relationships among the living are also served. The guest list proper to *misisi* specifically included an age-set mate, a *tilyet*, a sister's daughter's husband and his brothers, and, for each wife, her father, brothers, mother's brother, their wives, and her daughter's husband. These are all persons with whom there is mutual obligation and respect, but also a certain degree of tension. Thus, both the uncle to whom the host has given the "mother's brother" payment in brideprice and the new nephew from whom he receives such payment are included, as well as the son-in-law and father-in-law from or to whom the basic brideprice payments are made. From the woman's standpoint, the son-in-law is a relationship of deep respect. Little wonder then that the songs they sing around the beer pot are all circumspect, not vulgar like those sung during initiations, and the demeanor is polite and restrained.

This ritual was transformed into *mukutanek*, the new word derived from sharing. Though one family acts as host and prepares the beer, each has supplied some of the maize and millet out of which it is made. More importantly, the guest list is changed; kinsmen have largely been replaced by neighbors. These represent the new sources of tension in a farming community, tensions that derive from the kinds of disputes we have just witnessed and from the more petty everyday conflicts that are apt to characterize social interaction in this crowded land.

FAMILY RELATIONSHIPS

The Sebei household is made up of a man and his wife and children. If he has additional wives, each will have her own house, and the husband may have a separate one of his own. There are frequently other persons in the household. The man's mother, if she is living with him, will have her own house and will usually cultivate her own *shambas*. A grown unmarried son may build a small house a few yards away and remain a part of the household. A *mwet* may be brought in, usually a relative of the wife, to help with domestic chores. All Sebei say they want to have children, and women who are childless are looked down upon and will seek the advice of women who can cure them of their infertility. (It is assumed that it is the woman's fault, though if a man takes a second wife who remains barren, then they suspect that it is the man who needs medicines.) Girls learn early to help their mothers but boys are not expected to do housework. If there are goats, boys are expected to tend them, but for the most part they have little to do. Nowadays in the Sasur area they usually are in school.

While having children is important, I feel that parents receive little pleasure from them. I noticed that mothers with children at the breast rarely looked at their children and even held them in a remarkably impersonal way, encircling them with their arms but clasping their own wrists rather than putting their hands on the baby's back. In all my pictures of mothers holding infants, only in one of the twenty-seven instances was the mother making eye contact with the baby or touching it with her hands, except when this was required by what she was doing for it. I never saw a father handling his infant. Parental authority is severe, though not cruel. Any adult is permitted to chastise a child for wrongdoing. Children are expected to perform their duties and rarely get praised for their performance, only scolded for failure.

The relationship between siblings is rarely a close one. Though brothers belong to the same clan and are expected to give one another mutual support, they frequently are in conflict, as we have already seen. This potential for hostility is given special recognition for boys born to two wives of the same man at about the same time.

Ceremony for Half Brothers   One day we went with Psiwa to a ceremony for establishing amity between such brothers. Psiwa was presiding, because persons attain ritual status for a rite they have themselves previously undergone. The Sebei have a notion that the events of birth affect subsequent life. The first name a child is given reflects some circumstances of birth; thus in 1954 my young son was named Cheptekei, "born on a veranda," because the Sebei first saw him on the veranda of our house, and my wife was called Yapcheptekei—"mother of a child of the veranda," because mothers are addressed as mother of the oldest child, a usage that anthropologists call *teknonymy*.

Twins are particularly dangerous to themselves and others, and the parents of twins must undergo an arduous and expensive ritual, which I will describe in a later chapter. Boys born to different mothers are not twins, but if they are close together in age they will be expected to be rivalrous and are in some ways regarded as twins. The two boys may not stand together when they are circumcised, but somebody must be between them on the same cowhide so that their blood will mix together and thus make all three of them friends. Such brothers must not quarrel. The ceremony has features of the twin ceremony as well as similarities to the blood brotherhood ceremony practiced among some of the neighbors of the Sebei.

I will not describe the ceremony in full, but only the part that takes place after the ram is slaughtered. The scrotum of the slaughtered ram was pulled over a small gourd. Milk from cows belonging to the two wives, beer, and bits of the slaughtered ram's tail and penis were put in this gourd. Each mother brought her child, covered with a cloth, and sat near the doorway, the senior one to the left of the door and the junior one to the right. The children were uncovered, and Psiwa spewed a mouthful of the contents of the gourd on each child several times in succession and recited a prayer of peace. In the interval between repeated spittings, the older child looked over at the younger and took his hand, which amused all, for these two children had never before been permitted to see one another.

Psiwa then took bits of the meat, chewed them slightly, and put them in the mouths of the two children. The mothers then exchanged children to suckle them but the younger refused the breast, to everyone's amusement but to no one's consternation. A procession formed: Psiwa, the father, and the two wives carrying the children. Psiwa's son, for whom the ceremony had once been performed, anointed the husband, wives, and children with chyme, which was then smeared on the head, face, body, and legs of each person. The small procession went around the house, Psiwa banging an ax head against a pick head beneath the blanket that covered him.

MARRIAGE

Preliminary Arrangements   Marriages are traditionally arranged by men—the father of the groom, or a surrogate, or for second marriages, the groom himself, and the father of the bride. In traditional usage, the boy's representatives call on the girl's father during her seclusion after circumcision and speak his purpose only after being asked at the close of the visit, and then by circumlocution: "I have come to beg something from this house." And after further prodding: "I want to have kinship with this house." When the host enquires if he wants a bullock (in *tilyet* exchange, for the protocol is the same), he replies, "I came to see about a lamb whose tail has been cut." He should bring beer and might also make presents, such as a bullock, which ultimately becomes part of the brideprice. Such preliminary inquiries give the family ample time to discuss the candidacy and learn more about the family, if necessary. If the father of the girl agrees, he will arrange to have the groom's representative come to "break the sticks." The representative brings beer to the house of the bride's mother, where he will be greeted by the girl's father and a neighbor and such others as may be desired.

In olden times there was also bride capture—sometimes a real capture where the age mates of the groom abduct a really unwilling woman and at other times a connived capture, which is really an elopement with an apparently reluctant bride. All brides are expected to appear reluctant. Sometimes the girl's parents are angry and at other times willing. Her brothers may, for instance, initiate a raid on the *kraal* of the groom, attempting carefully to take just the appropriate number of animals for brideprice.

But whatever the mode by which the two people come to establish their liaison, there must ultimately be a bargained agreement and the payment of brideprice. The brideprice is necessary to legitimize the marriage and, more importantly, the children. We accompanied a neighbor to bargain the brideprice for his wife. He was a teacher at the local school and a native of Sasur, one of the emerging political leaders. The girl was also in school, hoping to become a nurse, but she was now pregnant.

Brideprice Bargaining   The Sebei bargain assiduously in determining payment. The amount varies widely, as does the way in which an agreement is reached, but a transfer of goods, and particularly cattle, is essential (though during the terrible years around 1900, many men agreed to the payment of only a few goats or sheep). Even for inherited widows or for a divorcee who is still able to bear children, at least one cow should be transferred. If the couple has eloped or if the woman has been captured, the negotiation takes place subsequently, but in the same manner and with the same presumption that an agreement may not be reached.

Traditional Sebei brideprice consisted of cattle, a sheep, or goat for the mother's brother, an iron hoe and an iron bracelet for the mother, beer, tobacco, and perhaps some cheese. Many other items have become standard additions. Cash was introduced at least by 1915, according to references on my questionnaires. Blankets, army coats, cloth for women's dresses, and aluminum pots were generally used in the 1920s. Other items appearing in the questionnaires include hats, *kanzus* (men's robes), iron pans, mosquito nets, lamps, kerosene, and *waragi* (native gin).

In my 1954 visit, I did not have the opportunity to participate in such a negotiation so I asked a group of men to enact it for me. This was a very successful device for learning the protocol of such negotiations, for it focused on standard practice, unaffected by one or another special circumstances. The men were conscientious in their performance. They had, for instance, two potential suitors and sent one away saying that if the other should be "defeated" (their term for not being able to meet the demands made) they would call him back. They accumulated a group of sticks about six inches long that were used as tallies. Each class of items is bargained for separately, starting with the cattle, then the small stock, then money and lesser goods. The bride's side is represented by a neighbor of her father, who initiates the bargaining by putting in front of him the number of tallies, in this instance eight, saying, "Five represent heifers that have never calved, one represents a cow with a calf, one for a bull, and one for the bull for the mother's brother."

The boy's representatives then discuss this and finally indicate acceptance of three heifers, the cow, and the two bulls but push aside the other tallies, provoking the response, "Why do you push these away? Perhaps you are not really going to come to this house to marry our daughter." Precedent is cited and discussion continues until a compromise is reached. These tallies are then put to one side and similar negotiation goes on for each class of goods.

When I had thought that everything had been settled, one man, who represented the bride's grandmother, spoke up belligerently from the back of the house: "Really, as you have judged the brideprice, I am not one to say anything, but if I had any opinion, I would not have accepted it." To this the girl's father angrily responded: "Why do you say that you would not allow this to take place? By what means do you say that?"

Grandmother: At the time that the Baganda came here, some women were appointed to go help on a job. We were all being made to carry things but the father of this man here saw me with a little girl who was sick and he went right on beating me and didn't pay any attention to what I had to say, and he didn't think that this little girl of mine would grow up and provide a wife for him.

Father: I was just a government servant and was doing that for the sake of the government.

Neighbor: Doesn't the government know that nobody can compete with illness?

Grandmother: My opinion is that these people should not be accepted because, though you have judged the price between you, they did that very bad thing a long time ago.

Neighbor: Truly, grandmother of this girl, if what you have said is true, you should have said it before the sticks were broken. Now that these things are arranged we should not send this man away, but we should ask him to pay a fine because he could not see that the child was sick. What do you think, Uncle?

They agreed on the fine of a heifer.

An Actual Session   It is by no means unusual, I was told, for such an old quarrel to surface and be used to demand compensation, but it can only come from the bride's side. Indeed, in both negotiations I later witnessed the issue was present, and so I was prepared for the way my neighbor's negotiations concluded.

Another Bargaining Session   In that instance the principals were among the more modernized of the Sebei; the groom was a teacher, the bride's father a minor governmental functionary, and the negotiations were taking place in a modern house with a corrugated iron roof. But the negotiations were highly traditional. They had agreed to pay six cattle (three heifers, a cow with a calf, one bull, and a second bull for the bride's mother's brother), seven small animals, two lengths of cloth to make women's dresses, three blankets, a mosquito net, a large aluminum cookpot, two shillings in lieu of the traditional iron bracelet and three shillings in lieu of an iron hoe, thirty-five hens, a five-gallon tin of tobacco, and three sacks of prepared beer mash. This was two cattle, a goat, and 100 shillings less than had been requested.

The bride's father, who, according to tradition had watched but not participated in the negotiation, then rose and made a lengthy speech:

> I think you have finished [the negotiations] now. But I have something to say. There is a case I want to take against these gentlemen. Here is the case: these people have snatched my daughter, and I have lost my year's school fees. I started to take a case against them in the court, but I have decided not to do so and to bring the case here. I had best bring this case here because, if you do not settle the matter even though the sticks have been broken, the marriage will not take place.
>
> I have sent my daughter to school for many years. I spent a lot of money on school fees for her. I sent her to school so that if she got married and then the time came that she wanted a divorce, she would be able to earn a living for herself. Last year she finished primary schooling and went on to secondary school. I spent the fees for the whole year.
>
> In the middle of the year, my son-in-law waited by the side of the road and persuaded her to remain away. He is an educated man who should know better. He could have arranged the marriage later and written to her, instead of spoiling her schooling.
>
> So you must agree on this matter. This is the only meeting place where we can settle this. . . . In all my years I have seen many boys and girls, and you never find girls fighting with their father, but the sons do. I sent my girl to school so she could help me when I am old.

The groom's brother admitted the mistake, expressed appreciation that the case was not brought to court, appealed to the precedent that a person who pleads guilty before a court is sometimes excused, and asked that the fine be waived. But the father continued:

> Don't think that I don't want the girl to marry this boy. I am only complaining about my money. If I could arrange for her to continue her schooling and get her certificate, that would be all right. A certificate would be valuable to my daughter. She may be insulted in the future because she has no certificate. Had she finished, both of these young people could be working and they could help their children.

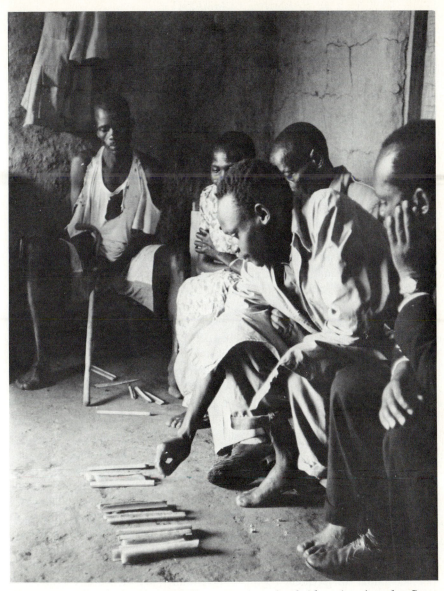

Photo 14. "Breaking the sticks" to arrange the bridesprice for the Sasur marriage.

These two young people are now good friends because they were just married, but later they will get annoyed with one another and the girl will be abused. People will blame me for not educating her properly. That is why I must have my money returned; it is only part of what I would get for her. If I ask her for something, her husband might fight her over it. But if she were earning money, she could give me as she wishes. I have already told you that I have been very kind; I could have taken a case before the school officials or the court. Therefore, I am not going to excuse you.

They agreed on a 450 shilling fine to be the first amount paid.

Not all the Southern Nilotics haggle over brideprice; in some instances it is a set amount. Where the amount is a standard *prestation* the marriage serves as a strong bond between the two kin groups involved, but where negotiations like those we have just witnessed occur, there is apt to be antagonism. In fact, the full payment is often delayed for many years and sometimes never fully paid, and this sets a tone of bitterness between people who stand in an in-law relationship. These negotiations only establish the basis on which the marriage is formed. The rituals that establish the liaison continue the adversary relationship between the two families and often reinforce a kind of antagonism between the couple themselves.

The Wedding   Some time after the brideprice has been settled, the groom goes with a close friend to bring the bride to his house. She is expected to go with a show of reluctance, bringing along a friend or friends, ideally unmarried age mates, to support her. As they cross the stream to her village, she should refuse to continue until her new husband agrees to give her a heifer. When she enters his house, she demonstrates her reluctance by refusing to eat and may well demand another gift before she allows the marriage to be consummated. She is fed by her mother-in-law and the groom is expected to seek a calabash of cheese, a great Sebei delicacy. If the bride really does not want her husband, she may have to be watched so that she does not run away.

The bride remains in seclusion under dietary restrictions and does not do any work, does not bathe or shave her head (as Sebei women traditionally do), nor speak in a loud voice. Some time later, the brother of the groom engages in the symbolic ceremonial act that marks the legalization of the marriage; he removes a bracelet from the bride's right arm and puts it on his and changes the one on her left arm to her right arm.

The ritual that closes the wedding rites, which may be delayed for many weeks, is the bride's visit to her own family with her new in-laws, bearing gifts of milk and beer. The procession—with the bride and her young helpers anointed and decked out with vines, the bride also covered with a cloth so as not to be seen—is greeted by the women of the groom's family. They are armed with sticks and engage in a mock fight, which sometimes becomes acrimonious, that ends with the demand for a payment in shillings. There are more demands for payment by the bride's family before she is ceremonially received into her mother's house.

Here she can voice her complaints at how her new kin are treating her—though in the instance we watched, it was her kinswomen who complained about not receiving some gifts that they felt were their due. It is hard to avoid the conclusion that these rituals exacerbate the relations between the kin groups rather than smooth them over, just as the bargaining does. Similarly, the demand for compensation by the bride when she crosses the stream to his village and again before she lets her husband have access to her on the bridal bed are not calculated to reinforce a sense of mutuality in the marital relationship.

Photo 15. Confrontation between the women from the bride's natal home (left) and the bridal party (right). The old woman holds a traditional clay-bowl pipe.

ILLNESS AND OATHS

The Sebei believe that disease may be the result of diverse causes: inheritance through the clan, infections, a condition created by rainbows or lightning, a broken taboo, an oath directed at the invalid's clan for something a clansman has done, an oath by the invalid's clan that should have been cancelled but was not, or an act of witchcraft against the invalid. A person who is ill may seek various kinds of treatment—native herbs or modern medicines, bleeding, or the performance of an appropriate ritual. When ordinary treatment fails and the illness persists despite the curers' medicines, a person is apt to seek the advice of a diviner (*chepsekoyantet*).

A Visit to a Diviner   Mwanga and I went to visit a diviner on behalf of his best friend and my neighbor, Charles, who was suffering in his leg and arm joints. That is the way it is done; friends go. Charles is a pleasant, outgoing man of about thirty without children by his wife of four years, a favorite around the beer pot, an avid dancer, and an energetic and excellent drummer. As treatment for the pains in his joints, he had been cupped and bled and had received other medication from a Sebei woman herbalist, none of which helped. There had been a conflict with his uncle over the land that had been given Charles by his father when he married, and the uncle had refused to take beer in Charles's home, which made him suspicious that a curse or witchcraft had been done, so he asked Mwanga to visit Samweri.

Samweri, the diviner, inherited his talent by belonging to the Karuma clan, which controls it. He divines with small stones in a wooden bowl that he shakes as he asks it questions and then holds in an almost vertical position. If no stones fall out the answer is positive. He was at first quite nervous at my appearance, since divination is suspect in governmental circles, being closely associated with witchcraft, but he performed the divination for us.

Samweri's questioning began: "I wonder if this is a kind of *mumek* [oath]. Spirits of Kapsombata [Charles's clan], please let me know if this is *mumek*. Please let me know what is the matter with that child who is sick. He has pain on his arm, wants to know if somebody bewitched him; please, my spirits, let me know what is wrong with Arabusi's son." He then asked Mwanga if he knew that a member of Charles's clan had killed a Gisu man and then went on: "So, my spirits, please let me know the person who bewitched this man. If this is *panet* [witchcraft] let me know. Please let me know. [Two stones fell out.]

"This man played the drum until his arm got paralyzed. If this is a disease of the bush, please let me know. Let me know if it is sheep or goat. If it is no disease, please let me know. [Again, two stones fell out.] Please let us know if Kapsombata people stole somebody's cow or ate somebody's goat or stole somebody's money. Please let me know. Tell the lineage of Kapchai, for this man is suffering in one arm and one leg."

Samweri then stopped shaking the bowl, rocked back and forth, continued, "They have eaten—killed a goat—father is clan member who knows—killed a dog and this dog was taken by a man, who killed the dog someplace where they hunted—dog belonged to Matei—burned the dog as one does a rat—must spit blessing on the dog—dog taken into cave of Kapenmet—this was cursed. That's it."

So Charles was suffering from a sacred curse that one of his own clansmen had placed on the man who had killed his favorite hunting dog and that, as is the case with Sebei oaths that are not removed when they have performed their functions, do harm to the clan of those who had pronounced the curse. It was to be removed by having the proper kin undergo the ritual of removal of the curse.

Mwanga and I reported to Charles and his wife what Samweri had told us and Charles confirmed the story of the dog's death and the curse made by a member of his lineage. His wife was much relieved when Mwanga assured them that it was not witchcraft, particularly after she had been further assured that Mwanga had not suggested the matter of the dog but that the diviner "had found out about it by himself." Charles never again complained in my presence of the pains in his arm and leg, though he did not get his relative to remove the curse as Samweri had suggested while I was still in Sebei. Perhaps Samweri's diagnosis had given him relief, since the cause was the more benign influence of a curse rather than the more serious matter that he and his wife apparently feared—witchcraft by his estranged uncle with its potentially dire consequences.

Removal of a Curse   In 1954, we witnessed a ceremony for the removal of a curse from one of the younger political leaders, a man who later became chief justice of the district court. A large, handsome man, he was quite evidently wasting away. He had been taking patent medicines and, on the advice of a diviner-curer, had taken Sebei medication in a soup made out of one of our white cocks. These did not help and he was soon taken to the psychopathic ward of Mulago Hospital in Kampala. In hallucinations he referred to two things. One had to do with bureaucratic matters. I was sure that his pathology derived from his fear of two powerful brothers who were his rivals for important office.

But the Sebei thought that his imitation of an elephant's behavior was the more important, and evidently they were right. They related this to an incident that had taken place when the Baganda ruled Sebei. The patient's grandfather had gone elephant hunting with a man of another clan and they had a dispute over the tusks of their kill for each of which a cow had been obtained from Swahili traders. The grandfather brought a claim in the newly established Baganda court and won it, but his hunting partner considered this a miscarriage of justice. He took the spear, some of the elephant's bones, and some of the earth on which the blood had fallen and used these to place a curse on his rival's clan. The curse was performed and the items buried in a secret place. For 40 or 50 years since then, a postmenopausal woman of the oathing clan had to defecate and urinate on them each dark of the moon. The curse was beginning to cause deaths in the clan, including the serious illness of the political leader who had not been born when it was first proclaimed.

Photo 16. Anointing the victim of the curse (in the broad-brimmed hat) and his family to remove the evil influence.

The two clans gathered at the home of the ill man, who by now was so weak that he had to be supported. The piece of elephant bone and the arrow were brought out and put into a special fire and the remnants later pounded to dust. A ram was slaughtered and skinned and the stomach contents removed. The head of the victim's clan formed a miniature *kraal* of fresh cow dung about a foot in diameter on the veranda and put into it some of the stomach contents of the ram, beer, milk, earth scraped from the threshold of the house, tobacco, and the pulverized remnants of the bone and the arrow. Branches of diverse plants that are associated with spiritual cleansing were tied into four little bundles, carefully using some of each plant for each bundle, and a stick from one of them was used to stir up the mixture in the *kraal*. All the members of the victim's family were brought round in a circle, including children and married-in wives.

Each of the members of the clan that had performed the curse took one of the brushes, dipped it into the mixture in the *kraal* and lightly sprinkled it on each member of the victim's clan in turn, four times on head shoulders and chest, while repeatedly saying, "*Anyin, anyin* (sweet), *baibai, baibai* (happiness), *karram, karram* (good), *chomnyot, chomnyot* (friendship)." A heifer was paid to the son of the man who had initiated the curse and a ewe to the husband of the woman who had last kept the curse alive by eliminating on the items that had been used for it. The former was spoken of as compensation and the latter as a fine. The victim, as I said, later returned to active political life.

Witchcraft   Oaths of the kind that we have been describing and that were punishing Charles are considered by the Sebei to be a legitimate and an effective way of obtaining justice. Indeed, many modern Sebei consider that truth is better served by this recourse to supernatural phenomena than by depending upon the witnesses that modern courts use. It is a powerful but dangerous instrument, for if not removed it can harm the family that made it, as Samweri said was the case with Charles. Being legitimate, the Sebei do not consider it witchcraft, which they know and fear. You will recall that Charles's wife was relieved that Samweri had not found witchcraft to be the cause of Charles's debility. Yet what witches do is essentially the same as what a man does when performing such an oath. So, at least, Sebei describe witchcraft; it is not something that is done publicly, and even Chief Aloni said to me, "For as long as I have been chief, I have been trying to discover who was a witchcraft person, but nobody will tell me." The difference is neither in the act performed nor in the explanation of how it works (the Sebei don't explain them) but in the social definition of the situation: witchcraft is an evil act done to harm others; oathing is legitimate legal retaliation.

According to Sebei tradition, *panet*—sorcery or witchcraft—is the most heinous of all crimes. But four separate diviners must point their accusation at the same person for him (I never heard of a woman being accused) to be found guilty. Then he must undergo a poison ordeal, which is administered at a special location by the clansmen of the prophet Matui. The suspect must drink an intoxicating concoction while sitting in the hot sun. If the accused cannot answer simple questions ("What do I have in my hand?" "How many fingers is this?") he is found guilty, and the members of the victim's clan will beat him to death, as his kinsmen stand by. I do not know when this rite, which has long since been outlawed, was last performed.

The Sebei credit neighboring Bantu people with stronger powers of witchcraft than they themselves possess. One of these, introduced, according to informants, by a Bantu-speaking resident in Sebei territory in 1938, involves causing some object such as a rock or piece of glass to enter the body of the victim. It is exorcised by inducing vomiting by a concoction made of a specific grass, but only two Sebei ever learned how to effect a cure.

A much more important form of witchcraft is *kankanet*. It is used only in retaliation against a person who has done harm or failed to meet an obligation and works only if the victim is guilty. This form of sorcery causes the victim to become ill by a wasting disease and can be removed if he rights the wrong he has committed. Unlike oaths, it works on the individual rather than on the clan (though it may work on his children). This form of sorcery is known only to the members of two clans, both of which are centered in Sipi, that is, in the area around Sasur. One informant thought it might have been learned from the Gisu but was not certain. The practitioners are known (or at least clearly suspected) and members of the clans involved freely discuss such activities. There was free and open discussion of the fact that one senior Kamechage clan man had taken action to recover some cattle from a son-in-law. The victim looked healthy but was actually wasting away, they said. He had asked his persecutor to release him and given the old man a goat as a token of his intent to pay the cattle. The attitude toward the elder's action was one of approval and respect, tinged with fear.

We had anticipated in our comparative study that farming people would demonstrate a greater involvement with witchcraft than the pastoralists, and we found this clearly to be the case among the Sebei. Not only do they more often express concern with witchcraft in psychological tests but have actually adopted two forms of witchcraft, one quite recently and the other much longer ago, both of which are more-or-less openly practiced.

DEATH AND FUNERALS

When I first learned that Cherkut had died, it was along with gossip as to who, not what, had caused his death. (It happened that at this time Gale had returned home to attend to matters relating to a fire that had destroyed part of our home. One of my friends expressing sympathy asked me, "Who [not what] caused your fire?") The Sebei do not believe that every death is caused by somebody's act of sorcery, as some people are said to. It may have been an oath (as we just saw), the breach of a major taboo, ill luck caused by the rainbow, or some natural cause. But the suspicion, the potentiality, is always there, and since Cherkut was only about 40 years old and died suddenly, witchcraft could reasonably be suspected.

Customary Burial Practices   The Sebei formerly disposed of the body by placing it in an open area and letting the hyenas eat it. Nowadays the grave is dug where they throw the refuse near the house of the first wife. The burial takes place quickly, preferably the day of the death. There is really little concern with the bodily remains, though relatives, especially women, keen at the death. The major rituals for a man's death are the ceremony of "chasing away death," a purification rite, that takes place on the fourth day after the death, and a final release of the widows from mourning, involving ritual sexual intercourse with the man who is to inherit them. The man's next younger full brother, or, if he is old, the first son of the senior wife is the chief mourner who "buries" the deceased, an expression used in ordinary conversation while both are living, as a means of pointing up the close social relationships between them. He is supposed to inherit the widows (though not his own mother) and take charge of the funeral rites. During the four days between the burial and the first major rite, the clansmen of the deceased are supposed to refrain from work and sexual intercourse. The widows are secluded inside the house of the senior wife under special restrictions in the care of a woman who is also a widow.

If the deceased is wealthy in cattle, his herd bull (*kintet*) should be slaughtered by spearing for the funeral rite on the fourth day. The chyme is strewn on the path to the stream, and the meat distributed in accordance with clearly prescribed rules. In cattle-poor areas, a ram may be substituted. The heads of the widows, the man who has "buried" the deceased, and other brothers and their wives are shaved; the widows must be shaved behind a screen, where they cannot be seen, by a woman who has also lost her husband, with tufts of hair left so that people will know they are in mourning. Ashes are placed in the widows' vaginas. All those who have been shaved file to the nearby stream to bathe, preceded by two persons who warn others away, as it is extremely bad luck for anyone to see them. There is a strong taboo against their looking behind them on this journey. The men go upstream and the women downstream to bathe, and when all are finished they return to the house of the deceased.

The Sebei use the emotionally charged atmosphere of the death ritual to make major decisions regarding the rights of the deceased: his personal goods, widows, livestock, and the indebtedness owed to his estate. There are usually but few personal belongings; these are smeared with fat and spewed with beer so that they are purified before being given to heirs. The spear and shield go to the senior son, the *panga*, or bush knife, and beer straw to a widow, and other things in accordance with private arrangements. After this has been done a hearing is held in which all claims against the estate are made public by the creditors, to which we will return shortly, and the inheritance of the widows determined.

The widows are joined in their seclusion by the man who is to inherit them. They are not to be seen, must not engage in work or sex, and are under dietary restrictions. They must sleep on leaves, not sleeping mats, must not prepare food, must not scratch themselves with their fingers but only with sticks, and are not allowed to touch their food with their hands but must use a pointed stick or leaves. These restrictions are removed by the final ceremony, a ritual feast that culminates with the man "cleaning out the ashes" by having sexual intercourse with the widows in the order of their seniority.

Cherkut's Funeral   Actually, as one might expect, there is a great deal of variation in how these matters work out, depending upon situational factors and sentiments involved. In the case of Cherkut, the as yet uncircumcised oldest son (legally a minor, by Sebei reckoning) objected to having his mother inherited by any man, wishes that very likely would have been followed had he been initiated. There was a lengthy argument over who was to inherit the widow. The proper person, the deceased's next younger brother simply refused—though, in the end, he did perform the ceremonial act of "cleaning out the ashes."

Eight separate legal matters were then brought up. One was a complicated three-way exchange of a goat, one a matter of a broken beer pot, and five had to do with loans or unpaid sales for which cash was demanded. These matters were quickly agreed upon. The only one that was not agreed upon was an ancient case involving the exchange of a cow between Cherkut's father and a Gisu man, a debt that was not denied, but that, the heirs claimed, was not Cherkut's legal responsibility. One of the claims was a loan of 100 shillings by Ngumui.

I was particularly interested in the behavior of Ngumui, one of Cherkut's brothers. At the time of the burial, he was watching Cherkut's sisters running and wailing and flailing themselves about on the grass in front of the corpse, and said with disgust, "What's the use of that?" But later, when they were lowering the body, he muttered something about being afraid and unable to watch and absented himself until the grave was nearly covered. When the matter of the debt owed to him was raised, he simply forfeited the claim. Here was a man who could not accept the cultural solution for grief and public mourning and therefore also could not take money from his deceased brother.

The Sebei use of their mourning rites to review indebtedness is an effective way to assure the continuity of legal responsibility and the allocation of rights and obligations in a population that maintains no written records. We will see how important this can be in the next chapter. But doing this also heightens the guilt and fear associated with bereavement, as we saw with Ngumui's negation of both.

Fear of Death   These rites give but minimal attention to either the body or the soul of the deceased. They focus on *death*, death as a phenomenon that in itself is perceived as a pollution. The rituals serve to cleanse the survivors of this polluting presence. They are replete with symbols of cleansing: general ones such as washing, running streams, fire and ashes, and the removal of hair; culture-specific ones, such as the chyme and fat of slaughtered animals and the use of certain medicinal roots and vines. Even the ritual of sexual intercourse (which might have been viewed as defiling) is expressed in the idiom of cleansing. I also believe the ancient symbols of Orpheus and Lot's wife—the taboo against looking back—are part of this context of fear of the evil inherent in death, not of the spirit of the deceased.

The concern with debts forces the mourners to act in ways unseemly in the face of death. These actions are not taken against the deceased, but against those who remain among the living, among the potential heirs, and between these and diverse creditors. Such conflicts directly involve the living, not the deceased, and provoke feelings of guilt and hence also fears of retribution. But the death is not irrelevant; it is the death as a social fact and a symbolic and emotional event that brings these unseemly actions into play, and thus it is death the abstraction, rather than the dead man, that is the source of the defilement. It is for this reason, perhaps, that the Sebei have an inordinate fear of death.

Perhaps also it is because the Sebei are very vague as to the fate of the soul. They have no clear idea about an afterlife, though they pour libations to the deceased clan ancestors. Usually these are referred to in general as the *oyik*, spirits, but sometimes they are specifically named. The Sebei view these as either good or bad, apparently depending on the behavior they manifested while alive. But even the good ones may be jealous and vindictive, and the libations treated more as placation than jubilation. Specific ancestral spirits may reinhabit a descendant, but this is not a general expectation. Sebei beliefs about cosmic forces in general are rarely articulated; the Sebei gain little comfort from their religion, as we will see in a later chapter.

5/Kapsirika: The
livestock community

Our house in Kapsirika was built quickly. For one thing, there were not so many people who wanted to contribute to its construction at two shillings per headload. Also, it didn't need to have mudded walls; we thought it better to have the air circulating. And our tents were more useful in this dry country. In direct distances Kapsirika is about 30 miles to the east and north of Sasur—and in vertical distance, nearly a half mile. But to get there by road one must first make one's way westward down the switchback road to the plains and then eastward for more than another 40 miles along the road.

Kambuya visited us while the camp was under construction, led by his favorite grandson as he not only was very old, but had been blind for 30 years. He had been the third man to come down to the plains to settle this Sebei territory, bringing livestock and his first wife. This was during the First World War, just after British control had curbed the raiding by the Karamojong to the north and the Pokot to the east by establishing a police outpost on the Greek River. These pioneers were followed by others, until the plains were so full that the people were just beginning to worry about who owns what piece of land. Small herds of giraffe, gazelle, and zebra were reminiscent of former days. At that time there was little landholding and less agriculture. Growing cotton was sponsored by the government, but giraffe are particularly fond of cotton plants and that added to the more usual difficulties of farming, and therefore was abandoned. Cattle herding flourished and in the past 10 or 15 years corn and millet cultivation has become important.

Kambuya was a rich man, though no one could tell it by looking at him. His clothes were dirty, old, and torn. His left arm was encircled with a simple iron ring of ancient Sebei manufacture. He wore the sandals made of old automobile tire casings that are the surprisingly comfortable and efficient footgear of the African bush. While I was busy with the workmen, he began to "toss his sandals" at the request of another visitor. The man wanted to find the location of one of his cows that was about to calve, as she had not returned to the *kraal* the night before. Kambuya held the sandals sole to sole in his right hand so that the plane of the sole was vertical and then tossed them sharply upward and let them fall to the ground. Each throw was expected to be the answer to a specific query. Sometimes Kambuya did not seem to like the answer, and he picked the sandals up and threw them again. If one sandal

71

Photo 17. Our camp in Kapsirika under the giant thorn tree.

had fallen over the other, it would have indicated that the hyena was on top of the cow and eating it. But one sandal was nested against the other, indicating that the cow had borne the calf and was lying down. If the sandal that represented the calf was bottom up, then that calf was black. On one of the tosses, the sandals were close together, indicating that the cow was not far away. The cow had, in fact, calved during the night and was discovered nearby.

Divination is an important element in ancient Sebei culture and throughout the region. We followed Samweri's divinatory effort to uncover the cause of Charles's malady. Divination to establish cause of—or the responsibility for—illness and death is widespread throughout Africa. The Sebei have many different methods of predicting the future: reading entrails almost always accompanies a slaughtering; the flight of birds foretells the future. Some things that forecast events are tied to individuals; one may have good luck if he stumbles with his right foot at the onset of a journey, another will have bad. Sometimes divination uncovers the cause of an event in the past, as with Charles's investigation; sometimes it predicts the outcome of events in the future. In both instances, however, it helps decide what to do. In our study of the four tribes, we found that the pastoral people were much more given to divination than the farmers. I believe the reason for this is that cattle-keeping people have to make more day-to-day decisions than do farmers and that these decisions have a greater effect on their future welfare. This is because the economy of livestock production is chancier and less routine than that of farming.

Shortly after our camp was built, we went back to Sasur and by the time we finally returned to Kapsirika, Kambuya had died. He was nevertheless to play a leading role in the most important event that took place during our stay in Kapsirika.

HOUSEHOLD DOMESTIC ECONOMY

Kapsirika and Its People   Kapsirika occupies a brush-covered plain that slopes gently from the base of Mount Elgon to the Greek River some six miles to the north. Beyond the Greek River are the much more aggressive and thoroughly pastoral people, the Karamojong. Their military depredations continue to constitute one of the most important elements in the Kapsirika environment. The area is warm and arid. Its 12 square miles of land is occupied by 279 persons living in 54 households that are scattered and far apart. This is 25 persons per square mile, one-fortieth of the density of Sasur. The average household is somewhat larger than in Sasur, reflecting the greater incidence of polygyny and the inclusion of people who are not a part of the nuclear family. In Kapsirika, of the 43 houses sampled, eight currently had two wives and another eight had three wives. (For comparison, the ratio of wives currently living with their husbands was 1.21 in Sasur and 1.59 in Kapsirika; the ratio of the number of wives that the men had ever married was 1.41 in Sasur and 2.17 in Kapsirika.)

The population of Kapsirika is not only widely dispersed, so that houses are usually about a half-mile apart, but it is also mobile. Only one in four of the male heads of households were born in Kapsirika or elsewhere on the plains, compared to 95 percent of those in Sasur who were born there or in the nearby area. The wives of these men show a similar pattern; 15 percent were born on the plains as against 68 percent near Sasur. The difference is even greater for the fathers of the household heads; only 10 percent of the fathers of household heads in Kapsirika were born on the plains as against 85 percent of Sasur fathers who were born in or near Sasur.

While the people of Kapsirika think of themselves as cattle herders, agriculture is not unimportant there. In gross acreage figures, the amount of land cultivated per household is greater than in Sasur. We estimated that about 250 acres were in cultivation, with an average of 4.6 acres per household, or 2.8 per woman cultivator compared to but 1.73 per cultivator in Sasur. But such figures can be misleading. First, since these crops are devoted to grain, they do not have the high productivity of plantains; second, since they are cultivated with the plow, they do not require as much labor input. Finally, the total acreage in crops is but 3 percent of the land in Kapsirika, so that

Photo 18. Drying grain in Kapsiriki. The white kernels are corn; the darker ones are millet. The kraal *gate is in the background.*

land availability is not an issue. We did find one land dispute, but it was not over boundaries, but over right of residence. The people of Kapsirika are somewhat less involved in the cash economy than those of Sasur and the major source (about 85 percent) of their cash comes from livestock, as against only 4 percent in Sasur. Men do the plowing using oxen; women do the weeding and harvesting with some help from the men. Each woman is responsible for her own section of the cultivated area and may arrange a work party for such tasks as weeding; but the *moyket* is by no means so prominent an element in Kapsirika life as it is in Sasur.

Livestock   We estimated that there were about 1100 cattle and 276 *warek* in Kapsirika. The average household has about 20 cattle, a little over three per person, which is not enough to supply the food necessary to sustain the people. The cattle are by no means evenly divided; the four richest men claimed about 400 cattle among them, while the ten men with the fewest had only 18 altogether. Cattle are kept penned in a *kraal* each night. Calves, goats, and sheep are kept in a small house of their own if there are many or at the back of the living house if there are few. They are all released in the morning, and after the calves have been allowed to suckle and the cows have been milked, small stock are taken out separately to be herded by young boys nearby. The cattle are supposed to be herded by grown men but nowadays are infrequently herded by boys. In Sebei opinion, a man alone can herd 100 animals, which should consist of about 4 bulls, 20 castrated bulls, and the remainder cows. Cows can reproduce about three years in four for 20 years or so, but bulls can service cows satisfactorily for only six to eight years. The bulls should be of different ages, or else they will fight one another.

Milking is the daily chore of women, both morning and evenings. Men will milk only in a cattle camp. Morning milk is preferred because it is sweeter and is specifically required for certain ceremonial uses. The gourd into which the milking is done is sweetened by rubbing the inside first with a charred stick and then with a palm frond stem to improve the taste of the milk and prevent worms, the Sebei say. Each cow is called by name and given the calf before she is milked. Calves are allowed to have all the milk for about the

Photo 19. Milking into a gourd in Kapsirika.

first week or two. How many cows a woman milks depends upon her husband's wealth; the men said that if she has 10 to 15, "She considers herself a proper member of the family," and that a woman can milk 20 to 25 cows, but the women told me that five cows are quite enough.

Sebei cows produce between one and two quarts of milk per day. As there are about 1100 cattle in the 42 Kapsirika households, of which about 300 are lactating cows, the production is roughly 400 quarts per day, or 10 per household. Milk is consumed in different ways: drunk as fresh milk; allowed to sour for two or three days; allowed to form into curds; allowed to form into a thick and ripe cheese; or mixed with freshly drawn blood. Milk is also made into butter that is used only for ceremonial anointing, but nowadays ghee (clarified butter) is also made. The cheese is made by accumulating milk in a large gourd and letting it thicken, pouring off the liquid whey, and removing the top mold before adding more milk. It is considered a great delicacy and is very rich; it is offered to special guests and to brides and initiates during their seclusion.

Blood is a significant part of the Sebei diet. Bleeding is done by putting a tourniquet on the animal's neck so that the jugular vein swells and shooting a blocked arrow into the vein to produce a lengthwise cut. The arrow has a blade, rather than a point. An estimated gallon of blood may be drawn at a time, and animals may be bled as often as once a month, but more likely twice a year. It is considered good for a pregnant cow to be bled, but one should not bleed a cow that is giving milk. Blood is important to the diet on the plains when other foods are scarce. It may be mixed with milk, drunk as a liquid, or coagulated and eaten.

Meat is, of course, also an important part of Sebei diet. Though the Sebei do not normally kill an animal except for ceremonial purposes, there are enough excuses to slaughter a bullock or a ram to provide a good deal of meat, and every animal that gets old or that dies is eaten; even the remains of a hyena's kill are eaten, if found in time. Nowadays, however, many are sold and enter into the Uganda economy through periodic public markets. When an animal is slaughtered, the meat is shared among a wide range of kindred and friends, as discussed earlier.

CATTLE EXCHANGES

Exchange Contracts   A man's herd is not the same as the animals in his *kraal*. We have already seen that the Sebei engage in a contractual relationship called *namanya*, in which a heifer a man owns goes into the *kraal* of another. There is also a second contract, a more straightforward way in which a man with too many animals or with inadequate manpower will ask another to care for some or all of his animals. The caretaker gets the milk and some unspecified portion of the calves from the natural increase. Because men living on the mountain in areas like Sasur are apt to keep their animals on the plains, the Kapsirika people in our sample were herding 1034 cattle, but they owned only 867 of these. The 42 men in Kapsirika had a total of 218

Photo 20. Preparing to bleed a bullock with a blocked arrow in Binyinyi.

namanya contracts involving 287 animals and 112 other contracts involving 420 animals. These figures indicate how important such exchanges are. It is very impressive to hear a man recite from memory 30 or more separate, often complicated negotiations that he had engaged in over a period of 20 or 30 years.

A man clever in the manipulation of these contractual arrangements stands to profit from them, as my analysis of Kambuya's herd shows. After Kambuya's funeral hearings, which I will discuss shortly, I asked his oldest son, Salimu, to tell me about the animals in his father's herd. He did this by starting with each cow that Kambuya had acquired (one was obtained by trading an elephant tusk with a Swahili trader) and following her progeny through the generations. These form cattle lineages, according to Sebei perception. They use the same word for cattle lineages (*kota*) that they use for human lineages. These lineages follow from mother to calf through time, and the Sebei think of them as a unity, just as they think of human lineages as a unity. An animal obtained in exchange (or even bought with the money secured from the sale) of a cow is considered a part of the same *kota*.

Before Salimu left the task, he had given me the details on 31 cattle *kota*, listed 559 animals (not counting animals that died as calves), 77 *namanya* exchanges, 34 purchases, and 25 sales, as well as 105 gifts or social payments. I estimate that Salimu described about half the animals that Kambuya had dealt with over the nearly 50 years to which these data refer. Kambuya's activities had been profitable. Fifty years after coming to the plains with but three animals, Kambuya left this world with about four hundred. He had engaged in three kinds of exchanges: *namanya*, outright trade, and sale/ purchase. In the *namanya* exchanges, he obtained heifers 48 times and only gave them up 29 times, thus increasing the reproductive animals in his herd; in trading, he gave up 18 cows (of which 15 were no longer productive) and got 31. In his 59 cash transactions, he sold more animals than he purchased and reaped a net gain of 4430 shillings. I estimated that he made a net cash profit of nearly 200 shillings per year while increasing his basic capital. This is only $28 per year, but we must look at this figure in the perspective of the ongoing Sebei economy, where the basic wage labor is 2 shillings per day. Kambuya's profits amount to nearly half the annual earnings of a Sebei common laborer, while he also had the milk, blood, and meat of these animals and built up his stock by eight animals a year.

Social Uses of Cattle   We must also recognize that these cattle were serving another more important function: they were used in *social* transactions. These transactions are essential to the basic goal of Sebei existence, the creation of a line of descendants. They are also needed to preserve harmony, create obligations, and therefore for a man to have influence in public affairs. Salimu listed 35 animals received and 70 given out by Kambuya, but this could hardly be the full number, since only one of the animals had been used for his own brideprice, though he had taken a fourth wife only a dozen or so years before. Of the 70 animals given, 39 went to his sons, either directly or as brideprice, 11 to his brothers, 8 to his only adult grandson, and 9 to other members of his clan. I think the best way to appreciate how cattle are used for this important social function is seen in the following example. A cow was given in brideprice for the woman that Kambuya's grandson, Chemisto, married; this cow came from a *kota* of animals that had been initiated when Kambuya's father anointed one of his cows for Kambuya's wife some 50 years before. Thus the infant that Chemisto's wife was carrying at the time of the study was in part acquired by a gift originally made by its great-great-grandfather.

This is, in fact, how the Sebei perceive these matters. I first learned this when a very old man was recounting the story of a war that must have taken place around 1900 and said he had an animal in his *kraal* taken in that fight. I was incredulous; certainly cattle could not live that long! He meant, of course, it was of that cow's *kota*. A man wants a representation of each of his sisters' brideprice payments, and of his father's sisters', if possible. They also speak of people in this way. Remember when the men were enacting a wife bargaining and the grandmother said, "He didn't think that this little girl would provide a wife for *him*." This continuity of lineage, both human and animal, is a basic presupposition of the Sebei.

A lineage of cattle is initiated when a cow enters the herd, whether as a gift from the father, a payment in brideprice, or an acquisition by exchange for something other than cattle. Her progeny, as well as any animals received in exchange for her or her offspring, are viewed as belonging to the lineage and as having the same legal status. Thus, if the dam had been smeared for a wife or allocated to a son, these rights would also apply to the offspring or exchange from such an allocated animal.

When a Western cattleman looks at his herd of cattle, his dominant thought is its monetary value, however much he admires their appearance. Though a Sebei cattleman also sees his herd as wealth, he sees much more, for the animals before him are a kind of résumé of his social life. Let us try to look at a Sebei herd through his eyes. First of all, some of the animals are his alone, to do with as he wishes without further ado, while others belong to his several wives. He can only use these animals if the wife agrees and the cattle will remind him of his relationship with that particular wife and the sons she gave him, for whom they are destined. Has the wife with many sons also many cattle descended from those he anointed for her years ago, or have the fates been ironic and been more bountiful to her in cattle than in sons? Some cattle may have already been given to a son, perhaps as a forfeit demanded before allowing his mother to anoint him at circumcision, and therefore when he looks at that animal, he thinks about his relationship with his son.

Then, again, there are cattle in his herd that do not belong to him, but are held under contract. If they are doing well, perhaps he will be given one of the calves to be dropped this coming year. Others are under *namanya* contract, and he may be reminded of his desire to visit the owner and enjoy the beer of his *tilyet* when the maize is being harvested, since his *tilyet's* daughter is about ready for initiation and might make a suitable wife for his recently initiated son. Good *tilyet* relationships, he knows, make for good in-law relationships.

As a Sebei looks at his cattle, he sees families of cows, each a distinct line like the men of a *kota*; each originating with some particular event of the past. Here is a cow that came from the herd of his father—indeed, it had been anointed for his mother as a gift from his father's father before he could remember. This cow of course is not that old, but she is the daughter of a daughter and thus is part of the same gift, a continuation of a tie that links him to ancestors from long before his time.

Another might remind him of the deal he made a few years earlier when he was given a single magnificent he-goat that he exchanged for a bullock and then turned that, through *namanya* exchange, into a heifer, this cow's mother. Perhaps he should really give another goat to the man who exchanged that bullock, even though that is not a real debt, but only a gentleman's obligation.

Among these lines of animals are some received as payment for his sisters and his father's sisters and remind him of ties to his in-laws. Perhaps a bullock recently acquired from the man who married his sister's daughter would make a good replacement for his old bull of the herd, but unfortunately he cannot use it thus, for it is not proper to keep an uncastrated bull from an animal received as brideprice. The bull of the herd, with its fine horns has sired many calves and is now growing old, and perhaps should be killed ceremonially. Could any of the bullocks really take his place? Such a thought may well remind him of his advancing years for, like most men, but particularly Sebei men, he fears death. And then there are the two cows he dedicated to the ancestral spirits when his wife became ill.

He also knows each animal by name, and—whatever its source, family line, or rights he has in it or has given to his wife—he knows it as an individual animal, with its particular habits, virtues, and faults. This one gives much milk but has difficulty in calving, that one tends to stray from the herd, a third is a natural leader.

We see, therefore, that a man's herd is a complex organization of individuals tied to one another in diverse ways; quite as complex as the community of people in which he lives and in many ways reflecting that community. His herd depicts the household structure, lineage, and clan; expresses the network of social relationships as they extend to his father's father and the yet unborn son of his son; and also reflects the ties that have been established through the marriages of his aunt and his sisters and the no less tenuous ties arrived at through contractual relationships, all of which bind him to widely scattered fellow tribesmen.

But our Sebei cattleman is not sentimental about the individual animals. His overriding interest is to preserve the herd as a whole and, within that, to assure the continuation of each *kota* of animals, for it is that line of animals and not the particular beast that stands before him and establishes his ties. Thus, he will trade, give away, or slaughter his animals as circumstances demand, for only by doing so can he build his herd and further his social ties. The herd as a whole stands for what he is, not by virtue of size alone— though a large herd is a measure of his success in the past and the nearest thing he can get to an assurance of his future—but by what it represents as a set of particular social relationships. In the final analysis, his herd is his autobiography and his monument; through it he will gain such immortality as may come to a Sebei herdsman.

NEGOTIATIONS AT A FUNERAL

The funeral hearings on the debts owing Kambuya were not held on the fourth day after his death because Salimu, his eldest son, was away seeking medicines from Pokot herbalists (at least, so he claimed) and this made it possible for me to be present for the extensive and acrimonious discussions. These give us an insight into Sebei attitudes and activities and it will repay us to take a close look at them.

Kambuya had had four wives, only one of whom survived him, and four living sons: two brothers by his first wife, Salimu and Andyema, one by a second wife, Ndiwa, and an uncircumcised boy, Mangusio, by his fourth wife. This complicated set of heirs, together with the intricacies of the diverse debts and obligations that a herd of nearly 400 cattle entailed, made it necessary to bring in elders both of the clan and the neighborhood to help make the determination of who gets what—to preside over the probate of a custom-based will. The drama that unfolded had to do with the conflicts between these heirs and the manner in which they sought their resolution. It also gives us an important lesson on the relation between established cultural rules and the way events actually take place—and therefore on the process of cultural evolution.

We must first look at Sebei rules for cattle inheritance. Actually, inheritance is not quite the right word for the Sebei feel that a share of the animals is a son's right from the moment he is born. How many animals this will mean depends not only upon how many animals there are, but also on how many brothers there are when it is time to take them. After a youth has passed through his initiation, he serves as his father's herdsman until the next son reaches that stage, at which time he is, as the Sebei say, "chased out of the house"—that is, given his share of the animals to set up a separate *kraal*. The last son takes the residue and cares for his father until the old man dies. If there are four sons, the eldest will get a fourth, the next a third of the remains, and so on. Matters are really always more complicated. The cattle anointed for his mother are divided among her sons only, so that Salimu and Andyema should have each taken half of these, and a fourth of those that had not been allocated to any wife.

There are further complications. By the time a son has been "chased out of the house," he will have been married. The father has an obligation to provide the cattle for his son's first wife, though these may be from those that had been anointed for his mother and they may or may not be considered a part of his share—certainly they will be if there are few animals. In all of this, continuity—almost a spiritual sense of continuity—is the central concern. After all, a man who dies without male descendants is "forgotton," as the Sebei say. Salimu and Ndiwa had each received their inheritance and lived separately; Andyema was his father's herdsman and shared a house with his wife in the same compound with Kambuya; Mangusio was, as already noted, a minor, and his cattle should have been kept in trust by Andyema.

While Salimu was still off on his mysterious journey, his brothers made insinuating remarks about its purpose, suggesting rather than saying that he was seeking witchcraft and perhaps was responsible for his father's death. Thus I knew that the *kokwet*, as the Sebei call any meeting, would be a lively controversy and I arranged to be at every meeting possible to record what took place. Ultimately, there were seven sessions over a 10-day period—and even then the task wasn't fully completed. These hearings had to accomplish many things: to kill a ceremonial ram and anoint the personal possessions so that they might be inherited, to find out what Kambuya owned and the animals allocated to the several wives, and to determine the debts owed by

Kambuya and owed to Kambuya and resolve the issues they raised. It also had to consider diverse nonlegal but important social obligations, including those to the men who spent so much time hearing these matters and to try to create amity among the brothers so as to maintain the continuity of the lineage that Kambuya had created.

Cattle Contracts   Just to show how complicated these matters can become, let us look at one single *namanya* exchange. Six goats were given for a heifer, three provided by Kambuya and three by Salimu. But the heifer was never received, so a case was taken to court and Kambuya was awarded a bullock. It was, in turn, exchanged for a heifer and again there was failure of payment, so a second case was taken to court and Kambuya was awarded a heifer. She grew to be a cow, but all her calves died and was therefore exchanged for a second heifer. This animal was given to a clan nephew to take care of under a loan arrangement. This nephew in turn gave her to another man as a loan (without Kambuya's permission) where, before she died, she had a female and two male calves (one of which was exchanged for a *namanya* heifer—again without Kambuya's permission—and another sold). These three animals constituted a debt owed to the estate—after two *namanya* exchanges, two court cases, two loans, and two cash sales, none of which had been recorded in writing.

The Funeral Hearings   Most of one day was devoted to hearing claims. Other matters had already been agreed to so that what remained were the more difficult cases. Let us follow one that was made by Naburei, a brother of a man who had been married to Kambuya's sister before he died. This relationship is not a close one, but he and Kambuya would call each other brother-in-law.

Photo 21a. Salimu (on the right) looking over part of Kambuya's herd during the hearings. They are pointing out which animals the heirs are to get.

Photo 21b. Men of the kokwet *discussing the disposition of some of Kambuya's cattle.*

Naburei (rising):   I am the second one to be paid.

Ndiwa: You have to prove your case.

Salimu: Naburei, our father took your goats and has not paid. But how many debts have you not paid to our father?

Naburei: I have no debts. I paid the bull back to your father.

Salimu: You brought a bull back, but the Karamojong stole the animal and you have to pay for it.

Naburei: I don't remember.

Salimu: There is another debt. Your father took our father's bull and promised that you would pay it, but you have never done so.

Ndiwa: Before our father died, he said, "I have Naburei's debt, but never pay him unless he pays his debts to us."

Naburei (with asperity):   All right, if you want to hide your debts!

Fagio (Kambuya's grandson):   You say that you have sent your son to collect an animal from my grandfather. I asked Kambuya about it. He said that he had sent you back, saying, "I want him to pay the debts he owes me first, as it was he who has taken my bull." My grandfather was ill at the time. He said that the person to pay that debt is Ndiwa.

An Old Man: We are all Sebei people. We must always tell the truth.

Kapsilut (an elder):   I can give you a proverb. A man may deny having killed a person, but he cannot deny his cattle debts. [This is a literary exaggeration; according to Sebei custom, no man can deny having killed someone, for he would suffer a fatal disease if he did not purify himself.] Naburei, you are denying for nothing. The story these people tell is true.

Ndiwa: I talked to Naburei's son and he claimed that if a man pays a heifer in a *namanya* exchange and that animal is stolen by enemies, then that closes the debt.

An Old Man: He is wrong. If a cow has been stolen by enemies, that is not Kambuya's fault; it must be replaced by his *tilyet*.

Teso (another elder):   You are quite wrong, Naburei. You must pay.

Naburei: You say that the debt belongs to my father; yet the old man never told me about it.

Salimu: I want to make this clear to you. This cow was asked by your father to be slaughtered for your older brother, who has died. Your father said it should be paid by you if your brother died, and so it is true that you must pay it. It is quite clear that you must pay us our cow, and then Ndiwa will pay you.

Kapsilut: All these sons of Kambuya who are sitting around here—have they said anything about Kapsilut's taking their father's cow? That proves that what they say is true. They are not giving false testimony.

Salimu: Naburei, you have two debts: first, the bull you paid which was stolen; second, the one that was killed for your brother.

Naburei: I will never pay, and I will never ask any more.

Teso: You say that Naburei has paid a heifer and that that heifer was stolen by the Karamojong. The heifer paid to Kambuya produced a bull and a heifer, and when the young heifer was ready to be served it also was stolen. You paid the cow and got one bull back, and the heifer and her mother were stolen; thus Kambuya was left with nothing. Why can't you pay this debt first and let them pay yours?

Naburei: No. I will pay nothing. I have lost and Kambuya has lost, and that is finished. What I strongly object to is the matter of the animal's being slaughtered for my brother, which I am being asked to pay.

Teso: Haven't you understood what Fagio was told by his grandfather?

Naburei: I don't know when they discussed all this.

Salimu: Labores [the deceased brother of Naburei] and Kambuya were great friends, but one day the old man's grandson seduced Labores's daughter. Labores came and took his cows from the old man's *kraal* by force. Kambuya took a court case against Labores, who was fined 5 shillings for taking the cows without permission and with this their friendship died. Remember? Kambuya came to you, and one of your cows attacked him. Do you know what he came for?

Naburei: Just to pay a visit—nothing important.

Fagio: Naburei denies for nothing. He has two cows and a ram to pay. He is trying to hide this debt because he sees that Kambuya is dead. One of the cows is a white cow.

Naburei: I agree to having taken the ram. Fagio knows all the debts belonging to his grandfather.

Salimu: Pay only one cow.

Naburei: All right, I will pay one. But please consider about my cow. I have been refusing because you have added a cow that was never taken.

I find it is difficult to understand; you say it was my father who killed it for my brother, and now you say the debt is on me.

Ndiwa: It was your father who killed the cow, but it is you who inherited that debt.

Eryeza: Do you mean to say that if a father had a debt the son will refuse to pay it?

Naburei: I want to be clear. Do you mean I will pay one and you will pay me?

Salimu: No, you have three to pay. Pay one, and we will forget the rest.

Naburei: If that is the case, I refuse to pay.

Ndiwa: It was I who was to pay you, but it is to Salimu that you should pay the cows that you owe.

This brief portion of the lengthy discussions that had been going on for several days gives us an insight into the actual behavior and the attitudes characteristic of this pastoral people. It shows how their elaborate exchanges entangle them in complicated interpersonal arrangements. Let us try to disentangle this set. There were four matters. The first had to do with a ram; we learn little about it, because everybody agreed so that it required little discussion.

The second was an exchange of a heifer for six goats. Kambuya had not given the heifer before he died; he had told his grandson before he died that the debt was owed, but that it should not be paid until Naburei paid both his other debts.

The third was an old debt. Naburei's father had taken a *namanya* heifer. She had produced a calf that had grown into a cow and should have been returned. But it had been stolen, and Kambuya's wives wanted that cow replaced. This is a rather fine point in Sebei law. Had she still been a calf when stolen, then as I read Sebei law, the loss would have been Kambuya's. Since she should have been returned by the time she was stolen, Kambuya's heirs argued—and were supported by the elders—that a replacement was required.

The fourth case involved an animal that Kambuya had furnished for a feast for Labores, Naburei's brother. Labores had been married to Kambuya's sister, but had died many years earlier. This seems to be the debt that Naburei wants to deny; he apparently resents paying his brother's debt. We have no way of knowing whether this really fell upon Naburei. The matter should have been decided at Labores's funeral, but no reference is made to such a discussion, only Kambuya's assertion that Labores's father said that the debt fell upon Naburei. Considering what we will soon learn about Sebei sibling relationships, we will not be surprised at Naburei's reluctance to meet this fraternal obligation.

Naburei expressed his willingness to recognize one debt and consider the score even, but Kambuya's sons were not satisfied; they will probably have to bring the matter to court. The Sebei do not like to wash out canceling debts, but prefer that each pay the other. One reason for this is that the heir to receive payment may be different from the one to make the payment, as was the case here. However, in this case they did say they were willing to cancel one debt and collect the other.

Before we leave this discussion, it will be worthwhile to examine one other feature: the rhetoric of the discourse. The elders, Kapsilut and Teso, take their role quite seriously, entering moralizing statements into the discussion and offering proverbs. These are, of course, appeals to tradition.

Sibling Rivalry   The central drama of the hearings on Kambuya's legacy lay in the confrontations between the three adult brothers. It is hard to keep in mind, as we follow the disputes, that these three men are united by spiritual ties they cannot escape and that, in times of crisis, they are expected to support one another. The display of animosity began with the insinuation of some dark ulterior purpose at Salimu's mysterious disappearance and built to a dramatic outburst by his full brother, Andyema. We can only look at a few examples, but again I will do this with quotations from the record, because they show not only the nature of the conflict but also the language of disputation. Remember, these were legal hearings before respected elders on a matter sanctified by a death and, though the elders had no power to enforce their will, the situation evoked the respect of tradition. Salimu testified:

> Andyema fought with Ndiwa and I didn't try to separate them as I was afraid they thought I would be taking sides. Andyema later came and objected because I didn't try to help him. And now Andyema is friendly with Ndiwa; but why should he be annoyed with me and friends with the man he fought with? Another thing with Ndiwa: we had a land case between ourselves and our neighbors; my father was my witness, but Ndiwa became the witness for the other party [his father-in-law].
>
> This case went as far as the district native court, and during that time we were very annoyed at him for separating himself from the family. The case was, however, decided in our favor. After it was decided for us, Ndiwa was asked by the other party to kill a hen for us and to invite our father and me and then to take the bones of that hen to bewitch us with. But we learned of this plan, and that is why we are annoyed. It may be he who caused our father's death.
>
> Ndiwa is married to people who had this land dispute against us, and Ndiwa built his house on the very land that was disputed. When he did so, his brothers-in-law came and took his wife and said to him, "You are a very bad person to build a house on the disputed land." So he went and built his house somewhere else so that he could get his wife back. Now, old men, that is how hatred came between me and my brother.

To this, an elder responded, "Always women! If you are two brothers, your wives will say all kinds of wrong things; then a brother becomes annoyed with his own brother, suspecting that what his wife says is true."

Salimu accused Ndiwa of sleeping with his subsequently estranged wife, and each accused the other of having slept with the now deceased youngest wife of Kambuya. This is more than an accusation of adultery, for to sleep with a woman you might inherit when her husband dies (as in both these instances) is viewed as a kind of witchcraft against that husband.

Here is another bit of Salimu's testimony:

Not long ago our father brewed beer. My father's wife had asked for beer to be taken in a calabash, and she took it to Ndiwa's wife, who had just delivered a child. Then Ndiwa and Fagio came back and said, "Here is Salimu, who has followed your wife." I became annoyed, and our father was also annoyed. I said to him that I had been here all the time and never went away at all. The next day they repeated the same thing, and so I got very annoyed and urinated in a gourd and asked my father to do the same, and he did so. My father cursed me so that all my children, except Chemisto, should die. Fortunately, the chief investigated and found that they were telling lies. Fagio was forced to bring water all day long, and Ndiwa was made to give a sheep. Further, these boys were enjoying my father's young wife until she died. And I am still complaining that it is you, Ndiwa, who killed my father—you planned to do magic on him, you had intercourse with his wife, and, finally, you took him to your house, where he died. At the time he was sick, you never supported him; and it was I who had to get the bull.

To this, Ndiwa replied in great anger, "If you say it was I who killed him, let us go over there to the grave and jump over it."

Both the urination into a gourd and the jumping over the deceased's grave are forms of oathing that will harm, by magical means, the person who is guilty. A person is suspected of witchcraft when there is reasonable belief that he harbors ill feelings toward the person suffering. The most obvious case of this is the magic that women are believed to do against men, for men treat their wives badly and these men have reason to believe that their women have a basis for ill will. I do not know if this applies to witchcraft beliefs everywhere, but it often appears to.

The quarrel between the two full brothers, Salimu and Andyema, was even more intense than that between them and their half brother, Ndiwa. It was a long-standing sibling rivalry in which the older and much more competent Salimu constantly denigrated Andyema. He usually referred to him as "this mere boy" though he had been initiated for at least 10 years and was a husband and father. As one of the elders said, when Andyema became hot and angry over a matter: "Andyema, I think that the way you attack your brother is stupid. I know your feelings; I know you think that Kambuya used to like Salimu very much." This suggests that the animosity between the two brothers was not merely over property, but was sibling rivalry engendered by competition for the love and respect of their father. I believe this was the case, but cannot prove it.

How Rules Are Bent   The manifest issue was over the distribution of Kambuya's animals and so we must concentrate on that. According to Sebei law, Salimu should have received no animals unless he already had an established claim on them before Kambuya's death, for he had been "chased from the house," whereas Andyema "had merely been given cows to milk" as he said. And yet the elders determined otherwise. For instance, one of them said—and it went uncontested—during the *kokwet*: "I want to say something about dividing the *tokapsoi* [the cattle that had not been allocated to a wife]. If there were many *tokapsoi*, Andyema should be given the most. If there were many, Ndiwa would take four, and Salimu four, and Andyema and Mangusio six—but Andyema should be in charge of those of Mangusio. If there are few, then it is all right if each takes one."

Yet, in the end even this incorrectly modified version of traditional rule was not followed; in fact, Salimu got nine of those divided, Andyema eight, Ndiwa six, and five were held for Mangusio. Andyema resented this treatment, probably as much out of envy as out of covetousness. At one point he shouted: "What I mean to say is that Salimu has been given his cows and is gone, and that our father is kind enough to give him more cows. Do you mean to say that when our father is dead we divide out the cows as if none of us were married?" Shortly afterward, he left the meeting, sulking. Some time later he returned, giving a long, detailed and apparently accurate account of Salimu having wrongfully beaten him, for which Salimu was severely condemned by the elders.

Nevertheless, Salimu's will prevailed. How did he accomplish this? Not because he was most favorably situated, for though in Sebei society to be older is to be more powerful, other factors could have outweighed this. First, Andyema had the legal advantage, since Salimu had already received his share of the animals. Second, as Kambuya's herdsman, Andyema should have known most about the current status and condition of each animal. This is where he failed. As Ndiwa said, "Andyema, you were misbehaving when our father was alive. You don't know about these debts. Salimu and I have been with my father; if you had talked to him and listened, you would be the one to know these things." This was also expressed by one of the elders, who quoted Kambuya as having said shortly before he died: "Salimu respects me, but Andyema does not, and if he were not my real son from my own stomach I would send him away. Salimu collects the debts, and this boy does nothing. If there is a law case, it is Salimu who takes it, and Andyema is only a witness. If I die, the only person who knows my cows, inside the *kraal* and outside, is Salimu. It is up to these boys to look to Salimu as their head, and Salimu should divide these cows."

Salimu's detailed knowledge of all these complex matters, which neither Andyema nor Ndiwa had, made the elders respect and listen to him. Salimu's remarkable memory was demonstrated to me when he listed 559 animals in 31 *kotas* of cows, together with 241 transactions they had been involved in. We have seen how complicated these transactions can be. The value of such a memory for a people who have no writing is very great. Salimu may occasionally have erred, but I have no doubt that the information was highly accurate because it was internally consistent. I am not suggesting that Salimu was necessarily smarter than his brothers, though he certainly may have been endowed with a better memory, but only that he was intensely keen with respect to matters of livestock trading and, like his father whose favorite he apparently had been, anxious to build and preserve the riches encapsulated in the herd. He was a true cattleman.

Not all men are so avid. Consider the case of Nablesa, a nephew whom Kambuya called son, and who "buried" Kambuya. His father from time to time insisted that Nablesa had the right to a cow in Kambuya's legacy, which Nablesa each time denied. For reasons I do not understand, Nablesa wanted neither cattle nor wife, though he had once been married. His denial of this central cultural value reminds us of the important fact that people in tribal societies vary in their interests and aspirations just as among us. It reminds us also of the reaction and behavior of Ngumui at the funeral in Sasur.

WITCHCRAFT AND FAMILY RELATIONS

Co-wife Accusation: 1   An undercurrent of witchcraft accusation was displayed in the discourse over cattle. From the reactions of the people, I do not think these were serious accusations, but only an effort at character assassination in the polemics of disputation. A more serious dispute also involving Salimu and his family occurred that brought about a second *kokwet*. This was an accusation made by Tengedyes, a sister of Kambuya. Even when Tengedyes was still a young widow she was apparently so cantankerous that nobody wanted to inherit her, and Kambuya took her in and made her two young daughters his wards. One of these daughters had recently become the second wife of a rather wealthy man, though the formal brideprice negotiations had not yet taken place. Tengedyes was accusing her daughter's co-wife of planning to engage in witchcraft against her daughter, Sibora.

Tengedyes had called Sibora home and kept her there because she had heard rumors that the senior wife had objected to the second marriage, had run away to her home on the mountain (near Sasur) where she was seeking witchcraft substance, and had tried to commit suicide by stabbing herself. The evidence that she was intending to do witchcraft was mere rumor and quickly perceived as such. In fact, the evidence of ill will between the two wives was overridden by their having cooperated in their cultivation of *shambas*, and they both denied having jealousy. The matter of witchcraft was seen as totally unsubstantiated, and the result was mainly moralizing, preaching at the two women. Yet beer would have to be brewed and shared to remove the animosity that the issue had created between the two families. I believe that the whole issue was raised by old Tengedyes as an attention-getting mechanism and also, very probably, to set the stage for demanding a fine when the marriage relationship was to be formalized by "breaking the sticks."

Co-wife Accusation: 2   A confrontation between co-wives that had taken place near Sasur was, in contrast, not nearly so benign. The junior wife was being harassed by the *oyik* of her co-wife's clan. The senior wife was a Gisu. The junior wife described her experience with the spirits as follows:

At night I have bells ringing in my ears; people tell me it is the *oyik*. The *oyik* don't allow me to eat—I can take only three bites of plantain porridge. When I get the lamp ready at night, I can see shapes coming toward me and going around and around on the wall and on the roof, and they tell me this is the *oyik*, too. I never have seen these things before. The people tell me they are Gisu spirits. At night, I hear the *oyik* running outside and I know I am going to die. One day I bought beer and sprinkled it around the house for the *oyik*, but that night they came and beat me all night and in the morning I vomited blood. Also some *oyik* had intercourse with me. I can't sleep; the *oyik* come and say, "Wake up! Wake up!" When I sleep in the house, my feet become swollen and my head very hot. If I sleep elsewhere, I am also very afraid but the *oyik* came only once to where I sleep and it feels a little better. When I sleep in my own house, it feels very cold at dawn and I cannot pull my bedclothes over me because my hands are shaking with fear.

We went to the ritual designed to chase away these evil spirits. The complaints of the women were heard before the rite took place. There were many involvements, aside from accusations of witchcraft, including a fire that burned down the senior wife's house, for which arson was suspected, the inequitable distribution of a collaborative harvest, and the failure of their husband to provide a plantain *shamba* for his junior wife. It was this last that the *kokwet* saw as the root difficulty and demanded that the husband rectify. They did not give credence to the witchcraft accusation. The woman claimed that her co-wife "jumped over" her sick child—an act that is done over a slain enemy and is believed to be done by persons performing witchcraft. But when she admitted that the child actually got well afterward, one of the men said that her co-wife must have done a good thing, because "after she jumped over the child, it recovered."

The failure to provide land for the junior wife was certainly a major issue and one that, theoretically at least, had a solution. But it was not the whole story. The following shows that there was little love between the junior wife and her husband.

Husband: I know the behavior of both my wives. My first wife, when we have a quarrel and fight, soon after the quarrel we can cook food and enjoy it, and anyone who comes in would not be able to tell that we had been fighting. But if I quarrel with my junior wife she never leaves that fight. Even after six months she still discusses it. If later I again quarrel, she goes on reminding me what happened before.

It happened that I was coming to Kamudei's house during the night and I passed here and saw something white in the bush with my wife. I forgot that man and we all came into my house. Still I forgave her for this, because I am a Christian. So I don't like a person to go on being annoyed for a long period of time. She is the only one who is misbehaving herself.

Junior wife: You have blamed me, but you neglect me. You don't eat my food or sleep in my house. You have told me you do not love me. Yes, I did that, because you neglected me and told me I should look for another husband.

The relationship between co-wives is not always fraught with difficulties; often they cooperate. The three wives of one man were collaborating in refusing sex to their husband because he was engaging in an affair with another woman. Women differ in their feelings about polygyny. Attitudes toward co-wives were as often friendly as hostile. One woman said of her junior wife: "I just saw him coming with her one day, and we became friends and love one another." Another wanted her husband to have another wife, but they were too poor to buy one, and a third claimed she had selected her husband's second wife.

A man is not supposed to play favorites; he should treat each equitably with respect to land, cattle, and personal attention. Neglect of the last may cause a woman to complain that "her roof always leaks," having reference to her continuing menstruation. Some women are accused of having love magic that makes her the favorite wife, but its use is considered very wrong. The first wife is supposed to take the role in subsequent marriages that the husband's mother plays in the wedding rituals of a first marriage and to instruct junior wives in their household duties. When a man is sick, he is to be treated in the house of his senior wife, and if he dies, she is the chief mourner. Wives are expected to collaborate on domestic chores but operate separate establishments. Each has her own house, milks her own cows, cultivates her own *shambas*, and cares for her children. Each is legally and economically directly concerned with the husband and their mutual interdependence derives from their common interest in him. For the welfare of her children each wife must establish her subsidiary rights to cattle and land, and because of such interest, demands gifts from her husband and his family during the wedding and whenever else the opportunity arises.

WARFARE

The Sebei plains were reoccupied when the British established a military post there about 1914 that reduced the incidence of raiding. But military operations never entirely disappeared and again became a major hazard with the end of the colonial era. As we will see shortly, Uganda's independence was initiated with a heightened concern over raiding.

Traditional Warfare As mentioned in an earlier chapter, Sebei military operations had long ago become defensive. They seldom initiated raids and frequently hid in their caves from enemies. But they did engage in warfare. Each *pororyet* remained independent in military action, joining others in battle only when it felt its interests were at stake and, indeed, sometimes even attacked one another. The Sebei were raided repeatedly by the pastoral peoples to the north and east, bloody raids in which women and children were killed and the population much reduced. From the west came efforts to take away the land and the Gisu pushed the Sebei out of some of their territory. Another tribe, the Teso, were successfully repulsed in their effort to take land.

Each *pororyet* had its own military leader. These were men who had proved themselves to be good warriors and who had the qualities of leadership. Such men usually bore the shoulder cicatrices that indicated they had killed men in battle. The leader consulted with the oracular power of the prophets and interpreted their "orders," determined tactics, maintained order, and led in battle. He was also expected to maintain an attitude of battle readiness during times of peace. In those days, the men were called to arms by the blowing of a kudu horn trumpet, medicine was smeared on the soldiers to make them invincible and render the enemy's spears useless. Some men used a medicine that was said to make them brave. Taken through the nostrils, it made men so fearless that they would go right up to the enemy in an intensified emotional state, with strong feelings of resentment and heightened physical ability. Such men were apt to be killed in battle, it was said.

The conduct of warfare varied: defensive tactics, secret night raids, or pitched battles. In the more organized expeditions, the men formed into separate units, older men staying in a base camp and younger ones leading the foray. Men with shields and spears would be interspersed with bowmen. Enemy spears that missed their mark were often picked up and used as weapons. Arrows were sometimes tipped with poison. Pitched battles would start in the morning and last until midafternoon, when, it was said, "Everybody is really very tired and both sides start blowing their horns to stop the fighting until the next day." Women sometimes accompanied men to battle to urge the warriors on: "I think you are becoming a woman"; "If you are afraid of fighting, let us change the sexes"; "You are losing our country by letting the enemies come in." Sometimes women went out in front, and then the men had to go forward, or they would be shamed before their wives. Spears or shields were taken as trophies, but not parts of slain bodies.

A warrior who had killed an enemy was decorated with cicatrices cut in five rows across the shoulder from the right shoulder to the breast; if he killed a second man, the scars were continued down the back; if a third man, the scars were placed under the arm. A warrior who had killed a man was honored in other ways, such as by privileges around the beer pot. He must, however, undergo a cleansing ceremony to avoid a disease that causes such severe itching that he will scratch himself to death.

Modern Warfare   Such warfare is now only a fading memory, but raiding continues despite the presence of a police contingent. The people of Kapsirika and the other plains communities must constantly be on the lookout for raiding parties. It was rumored that Chemisto, Kambuya's grandson, had speared an enemy to death. The fear of raids from across the Kenya border intensified as Uganda approached its independence, under the theory that raiders would take advantage of the distraction caused by the independence celebrations in 1962. Leaders from Kapsirika and nearby villages organized a bivouac on the banks of the Sundet River, just north of our camp, in which most of the young men and a number of the elders spent several days and nights.

The men who gathered practiced with bows and spears in an air of excitement and bravado. A kind of machismo emerged; the men stripping to shorts and a cloth tied across their shoulders. There was a good deal of sexual and scatological talk as well—condemning men who just wanted to go home to their wives or whose bowels were full because they had eaten plantains or maize mush and not just milk and meat, as warriors should. They insisted on having meat, and after long discussion, Salimu, the son of Kambuya, gave a heifer that was exchanged with his brother Andyema for a bullock that was slaughtered and roasted after a favorable augury had been made on the entrails. The next night they had to force another elder to furnish a bullock.

Patrols were formed to search out raiders, but the elders complained that they were "as noisy as boys chasing bush pigs." The third night, despite the patrols, a group of Pokot succeeded in taking all the animals from the herd of Kilele. I joined the group that tried to track them down, but the trail was lost crossing Greek River and when after dawn the spoor was again found, it ran through a Karamojong *kraal* and the spoor was lost among the cattle tracks. The owner of the *kraal* greeted us with an air of innocence.

The people of Kapsirika still value military prowess and find it honorable, but they have lost the knack, skills, and organization to be an effective fighting force. Even the will to fight is lost among the people on the mountain. They ran to hide when a false rumor of a raid reached them and they often condemn the people settled on the plains for their foolishness in living in so hazardous an area.

This absence of a military readiness has had consequences for the future of these plains dwelling Sebei. When I returned for a brief visit to Sebei in 1972, in the midst of the period of Amin's rule of Uganda, the whole plains area between the police station in the west and the military garrison to the east had been abandoned. Many men had been killed, many had fled up the mountain, others had relocated in the shadow of the police station. There was no trace of the 54 houses in Kapsirika and the land had returned to the bush as fodder for game animals.

THE KAPSIRIKA COMMUNITY

While the militaristic activities showed that the Sebei on the plains had lost their ability to fight, it demonstrated a commendable community spirit. I never saw evidence of comparable public activity involving the people in Sasur or elsewhere on the escarpment. I believe it would have been quite impossible to evoke such action there. This difference in community attitude is all the more surprising since the population of Kapsirika was an agglomeration of people from all over, even from related Kenyan tribes, while most of the men in Sasur were at least second-generation residents of the community.

Perhaps the presence of an external adversary reinforces this sense of community. It was displayed a second time, also in relation to the raiding activity. Kilele, whose cattle were taken in the raid mentioned above, accused Megawit, who had a Pokot wife, of aiding the Pokot in this action. It was the second raid on Kilele's *kraal* during the year. Kilele was furious and he made public the idea that he wanted to curse Megawit. Most of the men of Kapsirika gathered at Kilele's house and he reiterated his request: "I can't really prove Megawit stole my cattle or planned to arrange for thieves to take them. The only thing I believe, and that must be discussed, is that my cows have been stolen from time to time. Is this the only *kraal* where they can find cows? Let us find out what to do to help me—whether to curse people. But my main point is to fill a new gourd with beer, defecate into it, and by that the man who did this act should not live for more than a month. If this is done, I want the suspected person to be present, and I will break it and he will break it. The next day we will crush the gourd and say that whoever is wrong will die on that gourd."

Now this is the kind of oath that can damage any person of the clan— Megawit's if he is guilty and Kilele's if he is not. Toboyi, a young man of Kilele's clan, expressed this fear: "If we break the calabash, it will be *mumyantet* and it is we young people who will be the ones to die. You old people are finished." This is the kind of oath that may kill any man of the clan, and Toboyi was manifestly afraid.

In an effort to dissuade Kilele, Seperia, the local chief, cited the instance of Kamwatil, who had made a similar accusation 15 years before and had lost everything as a result. Kilele was finally persuaded to engage in a less dangerous form of oathing, one that is directed, so to speak, at whomever it may concern. It does not work its damage on the clan, but only on a person who is guilty. In short, the sense of community prevailed.

These community attitudes were demonstrated in the tests taken by Edgerton. The Kapsirikans express a greater willingness to engage in cooperation and show a greater respect for authority than the people in Sasur. They also show more guilt and shame over wrongful acts.

6 / Circumcision

About two weeks after we first arrived among the Sebei, we were invited to our first circumcision. We struggled out of camp in the dark and made our way to Atari, where a group of six girls were about to be circumcised. We arrived at earliest dawn, when nothing seemed to be happening; a small girl was practicing on a drum and a few people were standing about. Soon a procession appeared, a woman holding a flag, the six painted *chemerik*, as initiates are called, and a host of others. The six girls went into a small fenced off area and lay down in a row in order of seniority, each with her own sponsor behind her, the circumciser and her assistant, and some other women —including my wife—in front of them.

Just as the sun broke the eastern horizon, the circumciser took her hand-beaten iron knife and cut away the labia minora and the clitoris of each girl. The girls showed no outward signs of pain, and as each operation was finished the flag was raised in a kind of salute and she was turned so as to lie on her side, facing the east. When the operations were concluded, they all went to a shady place to rest and later walked off to where they were to remain in seclusion for the next five months. It was for us a dramatic entry into the intimacies of Sebei life, and while we saw many more circumcisions, it is that first one that stands out in my mind.

The next day the father of one of the girls sent to us for medicine and we feared our forebodings about the dangers of this operation had been realized. But the girl rapidly recovered from her fever and, indeed, it is rare that a Sebei dies from the effects or complications of the operation, despite the absence of sanitary facilities. We were to become well acquainted with these *chemerik*, recording the details of the subsequent rites. In fact, I learned through the grapevine that I was going to give my Volkswagen as brideprice for one of the girls; after all, the Sebei could not understand why I had only one wife, when I could surely afford another.

In this chapter we will examine the cycle of rites involved in circumcision and in the next chapter we will review the whole range of rituals, those no longer performed as well as current ones.

PREPARATION FOR INITIATION

The dominant theme of the initiation is that of an ordeal—trial and proof of maturity. In songs and exhortation, in care to avoid evil forces, the central theme is danger. An initiate of 1920 retains a dubious notoriety through the song created when he cried at circumcision:

> *Chemokey was cut to cry the alarm,*
> *Chemokey was cut to bellow.*
> *As a cow seeking calf; as a cow delivering calf.*
> *In Chepkasta.*

Circumcision is the only major traditional ritual that the Sebei continue to practice. It used to be undertaken every five or six years, but now it is held annually for girls and every two years for boys. The ritual dramatizes the transition from childhood to adulthood and establishes membership in the age sets. Traditionally, the initiation started in the easternmost *pororyet* (Bukwa) and moved westward across the mountain. It still begins in Bukwa, but it no longer follows in an orderly fashion. Once it has begun, any five to ten neighboring boys or girls can induce their parents to organize a circumcision group any time during circumcision season.

The ritual begins with the decision of one or more youths that their time has come. Many press their parents to allow them to join and circumcision takes place at an ever earlier age for both sexes. Very few girls refuse the operation but some of the boys have themselves circumcised in the nearby hospital. Sexual intercourse is theoretically forbidden before circumcision, though much practiced. It was traditionally considered "dirty" to have sex with an uncircumcised boy and it is considered dangerous, as well as improper, for a pregnant girl to undergo the operation. But more important than access to more-or-less legitimate sex is that, among the Sebei, to be circumcised is to be an adult, to avoid the taunts, jeers, and minor indignities of being a "mere child."

Youths planning to be initiated get together and dance to announce they are ready and press their parents to make arrangements. A week or so before the date set, they put on the beads and dance costume of a short skirt and scant or absent top (they used to go naked) and travel through Sebeiland to invite relatives and others to attend. My wife talked to three sisters who were to be circumcised together; the girls had spent seventeen days circling Mount Elgon, mostly on foot, receiving gifts and promises of gifts from about a dozen relatives.

Instructors   Each initiate has an instructor (a woman for girls, a man for boys) who provides and administers the medicines; goes with them and instructs them in the dances, songs, positions to assume, and other aspects of behavior; and ultimately teaches them the secrets associated with the rite. During the cutting of the girls, their instructor encourages them to be brave;

after the cutting, she disposes of the severed parts and the blood, which must not fall into the hands of hostile persons. She must be a person who has a good relationship with the initiate. The instructor must be trustworthy, for failure to dispose of the blood and severed parts could bring harm to the initiate later on. A permanent relationship, somewhat like godparenthood, is established, and the initiates will address their instructors as *moterienyu* (my instructor) throughout the remainder of their lives. A man may not marry a woman for whom his wife has served as sponsor, for they would be apt to quarrel, and this would be bad. There is no special ritualist or priestly role in this rite. The circumcisers have no ritual role; in fact, most of them are members of other tribes and the job is looked down upon, if not actually despised. Women cut the girls; men the boys. They are paid for their task and must be paid extra if a girl is pregnant or a youth has shown fear.

THE CEREMONY OF CUTTING

The ritual of circumcision starts at dawn, continues through the day and night, and culminates with the actual cutting just as the sun breaks the horizon the following morning. Except for the operation and some of the secrets, it is identical for boys and girls. It begins with instructions in the taboos on their behavior for the next 24 hours: do not laugh, do not touch the ground, do not put down the long stick that each initiate must carry, do not spit on the ground but in a handkerchief, and so on. Then the instructors raise them up one by one and they sing their first song:

> *The circumcision knife is in the house for you.*
> *It is not for the slaughtering of a cow,*
> *But for your slaughter.*
> *The leopard is in the house in need of goats.*

Let us follow the Kapsirika group (which included both boys and girls) through the day. The events just described took place between 6:30 and 7:30 A.M. This was followed by a long palaver over who the circumcisor would be; two men from the Kitosh tribe were rejected because a boy had died after one of the operations. It was about 8:30 when the initiation party marched off in single file, going from one house to another, at each of which they danced and sang. In the early afternoon, they rested for an hour and a half and were given a few swallows of a mixture of milk and water to drink. After more dancing they marched off to the river where they were painted with white clay by their instructors. There was much teasing and taunting; they were asked teasingly if they wanted water, to which they responded with proper stoic silence. A large group of both initiated and preinitiated young people joined them and all engaged in a great deal of sexually suggestive play.

At sundown the group arrived at the home from which they had started,

Photo 22. Initiates in Kapsirika learning the dance early in the ceremony.

where the circumcision was to take place and where a white flag fluttered from a tall pole. As the initiates returned, they were met by the mothers with a song of welcome, a very sacred song that is a feature of many Sebei ceremonies:

> *Welcome with some bread.*
> *Where have you delayed until sunset;*
> *Where have you delayed until down.*
> *Welcome with some bread.*

After a couple more dances they retired behind the house to be given more instructions.

Guest Behavior. This night is one thing for the *chemerik*, another for the guests, a large number of whom had by now gathered. For the initiates, it is a constant and demanding performance of dances; they go from one house to another throughout the night; they should visit the house of each initiate at least once. At one point, the group went to the grave of one girl's mother, who had committed suicide a few months earlier. Some of the dirt from the grave was smeared on the *chemerik* and the father poured a libation of beer on the grave so that the mother's spirit would know she had not been forgotten, lest she cause bleeding or death to one of the girls.

Photo 23. Initiates in Kapsirika being painted at the Sundet River before returning to the initiation site.

For the guests, it is a time for drinking, dancing, general gaiety, and license despite the serious and sober central purpose of the event. The party in Kapsirika lasted for three days after the cutting, with hundreds of guests of all ages present. Beer flowed freely, and there was an unusual spirit of camaraderie. Normal taboos are dropped, and a man can say anything, "Even in front of his mother-in-law." Sexuality is in the air and often in the bush as well. Men proposition women openly though not always with success and, on some occasions, women approached me in a suggestive manner. Some younger girls, dressed like *chemerik* in short skirts and bare, budding breasts, were followed by a group of young men who sought to abduct them. One old man shouted, "You young girls showing your breasts makes one's prick stand on end; you boys go grab those girls and get them down." Smaller children ran about making sexual gestures and mocking the movements of intercourse. One girl of about 10 was crying bitterly; some of her male contemporaries, in the spirit of the occasion, had caught her and made efforts that she was not old enough to appreciate. One man yelled that no person who had had intercourse should be at the circumcision for it would make the initiate bleed excessively and that a child conceived on the night of such a "fat" ceremony would never become rich. Many of the songs reiterate the theme of sexuality: "Offer yourself that you may have children; what is the use of a barren woman?" "Open out your vagina that you may take the banana blossom." Many of the songs integral to the initiation refer to the sexual organs, the crimson buttocks of the baboon, or the secretions of the glans penis. Verbally, as well as in action, sexuality is strongly expressed. Of course, the focal point of the whole ceremony is the genitals of nubile youths.

Initiates' Activities   When the initiates are not taking medicine or stopping at one of the houses, they are outside the house dancing, and some of the guests are dancing with them. When the *chemerik* are dancing, they dance side by side in a line, with the others filling out a large loose circle. From time to time, the girls come out in pairs and dance back and forth in the circle, each staying on her own side and turning inward, describing a long figure eight. After some time, one or two persons, either men or women, join the circle and confront these two, and the four do a leaping dance facing one another.

During this time the *chemerik* are often tormented, warned of the pain and the fear, sometimes in songs such as the following:

> *Approaching is the daybreak;*
> *If you be afraid,*
> *Go join the Pokot,*
> *Go join the Teso,*
> *Tie up your heart.*

One sponsor said to her initiate: "My daughter, don't make me ashamed. Nobody has died of circumcision. It will be painful, but nobody has died. It is not too late; you seem to be afraid." An old woman addressed two *chemerik*, annoying them by telling them how painful circumcision would be, frightening them with all kinds of remarks, and even striking out at them. They responded, as they were expected to, with silence.

The initiates are cleansed with emetics and purgatives and a drug, said to make their eyes steady, is chewed and spit up their nostrils. Just before dawn they bathe at a stream and put stinging nettles on their genitals and march to the circumcision place. There they are smeared with the chyme (stomach contents) of a ram that had just been slaughtered by old men who wish them a long life, and then they go to be cut.

Boys' Circumcision   We have already seen the circumcision of girls. The boys line up, standing rigidly side by side, looking with unblinking eyes straight in front of them. The circumciser's assistant sprinkles ordinary dust under the foreskin; the operator pulls the foreskin forward and cuts around it with one cut; the assistant catches the head of the penis between thumb and forefinger and the operator then cuts the foreskin off. At this time the initiate raises his hands slowly so that by the time the operation is finished his arms are raised straight above his head. He holds them there until the

Photo 24. Initiates dancing. They have been painted and are about to be circumcised.

second boy has been cut, when he lowers them to rest on his head. When the second pair has been cut, the first pair sits down. They remain there until all have been cut. Their mothers and other women raise a high-pitched ululation, the drums are beaten, and relatives and friends run and skip about and begin to sing and dance. Shortly afterward, mothers with cowhorns of butter anoint their sons on the forehead. Initiates frequently refuse this anointment until the mother has promised them a heifer.

Photo 25. Initiate at the moment of being circumcised.

"CRYING THE KNIFE"

The unflinching bravery of the youths is impressive. Only once did we see a girl "cry the knife," as the Sebei express any failure to meet expectations. A tall handsome girl, the *kaporet*, the senior girl first in line, refused to let the circumcision continue. This raised a great hue and cry as the circumciser continued with the other girls. She stood up, her dance regalia was stripped from her. She looked forlorn and cried silently. Many people argued with her to lie down and let the operation continue, but she was adamant. After about half an hour the girl left, darting down the path, followed by the taunts and jeers and a few thrown sticks from the crowd, a haunted thing. A group of men pursued her, finding her in a tree threatening to commit suicide. They brought her down, and completed the operation, according to custom, with four men holding her. The men would later have to be compensated.

I called on her a week later shortly after the painting ceremony, when her body was still covered with the pale paint. She was living in seclusion separately from the other girls contrary to the usual practice. She was embarrassed but not unwilling to talk. She explained that she was alone because her home was too far away for the girls who were to serve her. Her sponsor, she said, came from time to time to look after her. She claimed still to be the leader of the group and presumed she would join the other girls in

Photo 26. Reaction of the people to the girl who cried the knife. The girls at the lower right are other chemerik. *The two taunting women in the center are* motoriyontets. *The girl at the upper right is due to be initiated next year.*

later ceremonies, such as the ceremonial release. I did not find out if she was correct.

We talked about her suicide threat. She said that because she had cried she felt life would not be worth living, but the men had arrived too soon, and she was now glad that she had not killed herself. She explained why she had

Photo 27. The girl who cried the knife, two weeks later.

cried the knife. About four months before, as she was getting water a young man had tried to stop her and she had refused him, and he was hiding in the brushes the morning of the ritual. She was certain that he had done sorcery against her. In this way, she managed to project the blame away from herself.

It would not prevent the social stigma. A woman pays several penalties for crying. She is not allowed to be a man's first wife, for her husband cannot fight in wars, as he would be weakened by her. She is kept away from all later circumcisions because she might bring bad luck to the initiates. She is also despised by other women.

LATER RITUALS

Seclusion   A period of seclusion follows for the *chemerik* that may last as much as five or six months, during which they are supposed to observe a series of taboos and are served by youngsters, called *mwenik*. On the fourth day after the cutting, the initiates are bathed and shaved. The boys' penises are examined to see if they are healing properly and to determine if more cutting is necessary. The youths are also lectured to about their behavior with moral homilies and are given instructions about the medicines that had been administered to them. At this ritual there should be beer and dancing, and the songs have more encouraging lyrics, as the following in praise of the *kaporet*, who is thought to set the tone for the others.

> *Thanks to our* kaporet;
> *Greetings,* kaporet.
> *Had you feared the cutting,*
> *Others would do the same.*
> *As you kept still, others did also.*
> *You are very brave.*

A few days later, whenever they feel sufficiently comfortable, the *chemerik* paint their faces and bodies with white clay and may now go about and visit their friends, but they are still under some restrictions. They may not walk on the paths or cross a stream, lest it dry up, may not visit houses except their own, which they are supposed to enter through the door in back made for the goats and sheep. Boys may not be seen by any married woman. They may not shave themselves, touch fresh blood or meat, drink beer, or have sexual intercourse. Initiates should not call an alarm, speak in a loud voice, or greet anyone. When two *chemerik* meet, they should greet one another by caning each other severely around the legs with the sticks they always carry.

I was told that the boys will bleed their penises with a thorn "to make them sharp, so they can penetrate a virgin." Formerly during the period of seclusion they engaged in stick-fighting duels and practiced spear throwing and other military arts, but this is no longer done. Initiates of both sexes are subjected to some hazing.

Hazing   The boys are introduced to the lion, whose roaring is made by a bull-roarer that they have heard during their seclusion. The bull-roarer is a flat bladelike board attached to a cord; it makes a roaring sound when twirled. Bull-roarers are used widely in tribal societies. The initiates presumably do not know the source of this sound. While some of the older men are operating

Photo 28. Initiates from Binyinyi being painted some weeks after the operation.

the bull-roarer, one or more of the sponsors hide in the bush with a representation of the lion fabricated out of a monkey skin. Each initiate is taken individually in the dark to face the lion and is scratched with bent thorns. He is then shown the bull-roarer. When all have been introduced to the lion, they are made to twirl the bull-roarer for a long time, until they become very tired. If the blade flies off the string while being twirled, disaster will follow.

"Trick or Treat" They are released from some of their restrictions by a small ceremony. I remember one crisp moonlit night when I accompanied the first group we had witnessed being circumcised. Baskets filled with a wild fruit that looks like small hard green tomatoes had been collected. The girls, their *mwenik*, and a flock of other children went from house to house singing a haunting song. They demanded of the women some gift of food, and if one didn't comply they pelted her house with the fruit. I had the feeling that I had seen it before, for surely this was an echo of our Halloween trick or treat. The food is collected for a later feast.

Final Rites The ritual cycle of circumcision closes with a series of rites. These begin with a highly secret rite that lasts all night in which the initiates learn the true nature of the "animals," followed the next day by formal induction into the age set and four days later a shaving ceremony that allows them to return to normal life in their new status as adults. The all-night ritual is so secret that neither my wife nor I were permitted to observe it and though we know its general character, we lose out on the details. The original purpose of the secrecy was to prevent knowledge from reaching the opposite sex and the uninitiated youth. One thing they learn is how to use the "animals" (a term used to include the medicines and magical practices) to cause fear in others. Secrecy is preserved by a powerful oath:

> *If you mention it, it will mention you;*
> *If you neglect it, it will neglect you.*

One man said: "Nobody ever tells, not even mad people tell. They may tear their clothes or eat feces, but they never tell." Initiates must demonstrate their knowledge of this lore before attending subsequent ceremonies.

The *chemerik* are also lectured on such moral values; here is the kind of thing they are told:

> First of all, it is I who am your master; it is I who have led you to this lion ceremony; and it is I who am your *moteriyontet*. Never insult a person's child; never be greedy for the riches of your brother, even if he is richer than you; never be jealous of him, thinking that he could die so you can inherit his property. That is bad. Stay in peace. Pray to God who created you. Respect your mother; respect your father; respect your grandfather, who is the father of your sons. Be always pleased with your children, your wives. I wish you to have many children, and these children will look after you when you become old. Remember the proverb: "The sperm is liked, the grey hairs are not liked." Finally never mention what you have learned here.

The girls' closing rite introduces them to the "leopard," the sound of which is produced by twirling a stick between the palms, one end of which is on the head of a drum. We saw the leopard being brought into the house when the ceremony was to take place in Kapsirika. Carefully hidden from sight by the surrounding women, the drum was made to roar as the women sing the following song.

> *We are attacking the leopard,*
> *But don't tell it out;*
> *Look after the leopard,*
> *For you shouldn't see it;*
> *Look after the leopard;*
> *For no man should see it;*
> *Look after this fanged one,*
> *That no man may see;*
> *Guard the side of the animal,*
> *That no man can see it;*
> *Guard the animal,*
> *That no man can steal it.*

Each initiate girl, when introduced to the leopard, receives two scratches on the forearm that produce permanent cicatrices.

Return to Life   On the following day an open ritual inducts the initiates into the age set. Covered with their initiation cloths, they go about 50 feet from the house and crawl on their hands and knees toward the house in single file, while the older women dance backward in front of them. The crawling is a form of punishment, the distance depending upon whether they have been misbehaving, and the fault of one brings suffering to all. They are then asked to identify their age set, being queried by an old person with wrong and right ones mixed, and they rise up under their cloths, assenting with a protracted "hmm" when the correct one is called. They are then blessed with beer and milk spewed upon them by the senior person, and anointed on the head with butter by their mothers. The girls are given new clothes and a dance follows.

Four days later each initiate is shaved, the hair carefully burned in a ritual fire. They are then instructed in the ordinary tasks of daily life: taking corn from a granary, using a hoe, grinding grain, peeling plantains for the women; shooting bows, throwing spears, handling the herding sticks by the men. The initiates are blessed by spitting beer as they undertake each of these tasks. They then may enter their parental house, greeted by the senior woman at the door and blessed by having milk or beer spit on them. They are now members of adult Sebei society.

VARIATION IN THE CIRCUMCISION RITE

This description has been compounded out of observations made in Sasur, Kapsirika, and elsewhere and from other things that Sebei told me concerning circumcision. There are, however, variations in time and space that must now briefly engage our attention.

Historical Changes   Let us first consider some of the changes from pre-colonial practice. First, the Sebei-wide coordination of the ritual and the unity of the *pororyet* in staging it were lost early. These changes relate, indirectly at least, to the elimination of warfare and the prophet. (The time of circumcision was reset by governmental regulation to minimize the disruption of the educational process. I have no idea, nor any Sebei explanation, as to why they began to hold circumcisions more frequently.) Lost are the contests, the practice of military arts, and other elements having to do with the age set as a potential fighting force.

Recent years have seen a further erosion of traditional usages. This has, as would be expected, been greater in the western agricultural area than in the east and on the plains, where cattle keeping retains its importance. To some extent, this has resulted from the loss of belief or faith in the unseen supernatural forces that must be respected and feared. One young woman told me that she had spent the night before her circumcision listening to phonograph records! An educated boy had resisted undergoing initiation because he thought it was foolish since it had been emptied of its ancient meaning and only gave in to his highly traditional father because he would be taunted as a coward if he did not.

Regional Differences   Aside from such differences brought on by outside influences, there is one important difference between Kapsirika and Sasur. In Kapsirika, the men who put on a circumcision for their children make a great show of it. Siret, who was planning the circumcision in Kapsirika of two sons and three daughters, said disdainfully, "I wish I lived in Masop [the area around Sasur] where the people aren't troubled. As soon as the circumcision is over, they just walk away to find where the beer is. A friend of mine who had his girls circumcised made beer, but when the time came he sold that beer and went out to find beer for himself."

He was not exaggerating much. In one instance we witnessed in 1954, the beer was less than social expectations demanded, while in another there was none. In Sasur in 1962, there was even less concern with meeting these social obligations. Only one of the six parents furnished a ram for slaughter, and there was no feasting. The father of the senior girl quite clearly had no intention of killing an animal or providing beer; he made no preparations for his daughter's initiation. This was not unusual; three men were tied up during the circumcision of their children as "prisoners" of their age-set mates because they had failed to provide beer for them as custom demanded.

Matters were very different with Siret in Kapsirika. A week or more before the date set he claimed to have already spent 4000 shillings and was accumulating animals to slaughter, laying down beer, and buying sugar in 100-pound sacks and tea in quantity. More than 30 men were to receive specific invitations. They would bring their wives and children, and many others, he was sure, would "push in." He described enviously the arrangements made by a rich man in the next village who had had a circumcision two years earlier and was planning another.

Koboloman had a circumcision ceremony, and we stayed at his house a month. If you had taken pictures, you would have run out of film. This time he has prepared 40 sacks of maize and I think he wants people to stay at his home for two months. Koboloman is very proud of himself because he is rich in food. Everybody respects him, for he buys respect in this way. Last time he killed six oxen. This man will brew so much beer he hasn't room in his house and must rent his neighbors' houses. When such a person is around the beer pots, people will dance and speak his name, tell the amount of beer, and say that he kept people at his house for such a long time. We despise those people [in the mountain area] who put their children together, select one of them to slaughter a ram, and after the circumcision get one or two pots of beer, or just buy a 20-shilling pot. Nobody in Masop tries to compete with another . . . so that he would come to be a person who is known.

Associated with this difference in lavish display is the prevalence of gifts to the initiates. While an occasional small gift may have been given to initiates in Sasur, the boys in Kapsirika received as many as three cattle before the ritual was concluded, as well as gifts of sheep and money. This giving to the initiates is certainly an old feature of the ritual; I am less certain about the display of wealth. That may come into play as a secondary result of splitting the circumcision groups into separate small units.

THE CONTINUING TRADITION OF CIRCUMCISION

Why has circumcision been the one major Sebei ritual to have survived the impact of colonial rule? It had largely lost its major sociological function, the formation of age-set unity for military purposes, even before the advent of colonialism. It had lost its secondary function of unifying the *pororyet* and the whole Sebei people early in the colonial era. A good deal of pressure against the custom, especially for girls, has come from both administrators and missionaries, yet it nevertheless has persisted when other rites, to which we will turn in the next chapter, have long since disappeared.

The answer to this question is not a simple one, and I can only offer some conjectures. First, I think the reason is somewhat different for boys than it is for girls. For boys, I think, it is very largely a matter of pride, of the unwillingness of youth to be taunted for being fearful. The Sebei do not hesitate to make fun of one another for their shortcomings, and I have heard men accuse others of having been circumcised at the hospital. Such peer group pressure, as we all know from our own youth, is a potent force.

Some of this may apply to the girls as well, but I am inclined to think there is a more powerful reason. First, we must not assume that it is foisted on the girls by the men. In recent years, there have been discussions in feminist circles about the horror of "female mutilation" as something the men force upon their women. There is evidence that this is the case in those societies where the vagina is made to heal closed or actually infibulated to assure the preservation of virginity. Among the Sebei there is no such practice. Some Western-educated Sebei men expressed to me that the custom of female, but not male, circumcision should be abandoned. Yet many girls press upon reluctant fathers their demand that the time for circumcision had come.

Female circumcision has two sets of sociological implications relevant to this issue. First, by the very fact of undergoing a trial fully as difficult as that of the men, women put themselves on a basis of equality with them. This must have been particularly important under the traditional circumstances. More important nowadays is the fact that female circumcision creates a sisterhood of women in a society dominated by men; it is a powerful counterforce to the mistreatment they regularly receive from their fathers and husbands.

Let us look briefly at some of the relevant elements. First, age-set distinctions are not important to women; the initiation really creates a unity among *all* women. Second, overt hostility was clearly expressed toward men by the women as they organize for the leopard ceremony. Third, what they are taught during that ceremony is magic against men—or so they say and so the Sebei men firmly believe. One of the dominant attitudes of the Sebei found by

Robert Edgerton in his psychological investigation was men's fear of women; the women admit that men fear them and with good reason. One told Edgerton "a man must treat me well; if he does not . . . well, he will regret it." The antagonism goes both ways. One of the male circumcision songs has the following lyric:

> *Our fathers have come,*
> *Have come very slowly*
> *To cut for me my spear.*
> *I shall spear my enemies,*
> *The enemies of my hearth.*

There is some evidence that circumcision for Sebei women has increased in importance in recent years. I was told that the leopard ceremony had disappeared in the plantain sector of Sebei before the colonial period, and older women do not bear the scars of the leopard's scratch. In recent years, however, the leopard ceremony was reintroduced and made an integral part of initiation—that very part of the initiation cycle that emphasizes the unity of women and their antagonism toward men.

Whether these speculations are correct, there is no doubt that circumcision among the Sebei continues to be the most prominent feature of their ritual activities.

7 / Religion

The Sebei have no priests. They rarely discuss their beliefs or speculate about either their origins as a people or their fate as individuals. Even their prayers are terse, often merely the words "sweet" and "peace," or exhortations to ancestral spirits to bring them no harm. What Sebei say about the supernatural can be briefly summarized. God is the sun, *Asista*. He has little to do with the ordinary events of human life, though He is the ultimate source of existence. Prayers are not addressed to *Asista*. *Masop*, the anthropomorphic representation of Mount Elgon, is the original ancestral being who sired them and the neighboring related tribes, each of which originated from one of his several sons. He is the ultimate ancestor, but not a god.

Spirits More important are the *oyik*, the spirits that dwell in a vague underworld and are presumed to exist in much the same way that the living do. They are the spirits of the dead. They are most often appealed to in this plural form, especially the *oyik* of the clan. They are capable of helping or harming the living, but the Sebei make no appeals to them for personal help. They are occasionally asked to bring a generalized condition of well being and peace, but more often are placated so that they will cause no harm. While the spirits of individual ancestors may be addressed in a similar manner, even then the prayer and libation is to induce them not to do harm. *Oyik* apparently fall into two classes, good and bad. Libations of food and beer are placed at the *kraal* gate or at the centerpost of the house for the good *oyik* but thrown out away from the house for the bad, with exhortations that they leave.

Ritual Though the Sebei say little about their beliefs, they nevertheless have them. Ideas about supernatural events are expressed in ritual. We must therefore examine the form and content of Sebei rituals to understand their perception of supernatural events and their feeling about them. Religion is not a separate compartment of life, but suffuses everyday events. We have already seen ritual in many aspects of Sebei daily life: circumcision, divination, oathing and witchcraft, marriages, funerals, and other events.

What is ritual and what does it do? Rituals communicate *feelings*. It is the counterpart to language, which communicates *understanding*. There are two largely separate spheres of human psychology: emotion and thought. In all cultures, people share their feelings about the world, as well as their understanding of what it is like. They need to have a means of communicating these feelings. While one can talk *about* feelings—we can say we are angry or in love—this is a poor substitute for a burst of rage or an affectionate caress. Ritual communicates sentiment in various ways. It uses pain; it uses fear; it uses isolation. It calls on aesthetic expressions—music (we all know how a melody can evoke a mood), dance, plastic arts. A good exercise would be to look back over rituals already described to find out what sentiments they appear to evoke among the participants; later, I will summarize them. The dominant and pervasive sentiments of a people can be reconstructed by such an examination of their rituals.

SEBEI-WIDE RITUALS

The rituals discussed in earlier chapters have to do with personal or family matters: weddings and funerals, ceremonies for brothers or to remove a curse, and the like (the only exception is *chomi ntarastit*, which was Sebei-wide). Initiation rites are also local and personal, though at one time they were coordinated Sebei wide and therefore also had a broader social purpose. The Sebei formerly had rituals, mostly called *korosek* rites, that expressed the unity of the *pororyet* and the Sebei as a whole. These ceremonies were abandoned in the early decades of colonial control; we know them only from accounts given by older persons.

Korosek rites were initiated by the prophet; he determined when they should take place and he selected certain leaders to organize the activity. He played no further part in them.

All the Sebei-wide rituals, including initiation, were begun in the east with the *pororyet* of Bukwa and moved successively across the escarpment *poroyet* by *poroyet* to the west. One of these rituals was *chomi ntarastit*, already described. Because it never was regularized, the prophet apparently did have a continuing involvement with this rite.

Harvest Ritual   The most important of the old *korosek* rites was a ritual held annually at the beginning of the harvest. The last one was held in 1928. The prophet selected three men in each *pororyet* to serve as ritual leaders, one to provide a black bull for slaughtering, one to light the sacred fire, and the third, who must be an old man, to cut up and distribute the meat. The ritual was held by a large tree near the house of the man who provided the sacrificial animal. An old man made the ritual fire with fire sticks that were not to be used again. He placed on the fire a number of branches and leaves of a variety of plants that had special cleansing properties—the *korosek* plants. Each of the women of the *pororyet* put on the fire some of each crop— millet, corn, beans, sweet potatoes, yams, and tobacco. The women brought milk from the morning's milking, milk from all lactating women, and a piece of firewood taken from the wood rack inside the house and added them to the fire. The content of the intestines of the bull was put on the fire to produce smoke, but the chyme was taken home by the women, to put a bit in their pots when they cooked the new crop.

All the people of the *pororyet* together with their cattle and small animals, gathered around this fire (men and boys to the east, women and girls to the west) and breathed the smoke. The meat of the bull was roasted and consumed, as no part could be taken from the ceremonial grounds. The skin was cut into small rings and worn by all the people; men on their right middle finger, women on their iron necklaces. The bones were thrown into the fire.

At sunset of the first day of the ceremony, the women took a coal on a piece of wood and threw it away with their left hand, saying, "Go away!" "They are sending away disease, famine, and all kinds of bad luck." That evening, they took coals to their homes to start a new fire in the hearths that had been cleaned of ashes. This fire had to remain for the four days of the ceremony and neither work nor sexual intercourse was allowed during those four days.

Disease Ritual   Another *korosek* ceremony was also performed to eliminate disease, as during the smallpox epidemic at the beginning of this century. This ritual involved the same *korosek* plants and appears to be a modification of the annual rite. It had essentially the same function. The prophet appointed a person in each *poroyet* to slaughter a bull or ram by stabbing it with a knife. Pieces of meat from all parts of the animal were skewered on two sticks and taken by about ten selected persons at sunset to the west across the stream that marked the *poroyet's* western boundary. There the sticks were planted in the ground, slanting to the westward. Thus the diseases were expelled from the *pororyet*. As the ceremony moved to the westernmost *pororyet* the people would throw the ritual meat into the Siroko River and say, "Disease, go with this water to the land of the Teso."

The purpose of the third ritual was to bring rain at times of drought. For this, there was neither beer nor feasting, but the people danced during the day at the pool in a stream where the ceremony was held. In the afternoon, a precircumcision girl—that is, a virgin—would enter a stream, carrying a palm frond and a ball of beer mash followed by a man leading a ewe that had not yet reproduced (also a virgin). The girl would beat the water with the palm frond and throw the ball of beer mash into the water, singing a song that asked Thunder to bring rain.

Plantain Ritual   One other ritual of more-or-less national scope was entirely different from all the rest. It was borrowed from the Bagwere, a Bantu people who had settled peacably in the western part of Sebeiland. This rite had a ritual specialist who belonged to the particular clan that owned the rites. Wearing bells on his legs and accompanied by a drummer, he went through the plantain *shambas* and sprinkled with a whisk a concoction made of 25 plants. The landowners were expected to slaughter a goat and give a feast for the ritualist.

The purpose of this rite was to assure the fertility of the plantain crops and, like the plantains themselves (but unlike all other rituals), originated in the west and moved eastward. It was never held beyond the area heavily cultivated to plantains. It too was long ago abandoned. While it is not really a Sebei rite and doesn't help us to understand the Sebei, it does give us a lesson in cultural change: the acquisition of an important new cultural item such as plantains is apt to include taking over the rituals associated with it.

CLAN RITES

The clan is the most important spiritual entity in all Sebei. All oaths assume that the supernatural forces, whatever these may be, seek out and destroy clan members. This invisible tie derives from the fact of paternity; a person is a member of the clan of the man who sired him. Of course, the Sebei cannot always be sure of paternity any more than anybody else, but it is considered very evil for a person to claim membership in a clan to which he was not born; this is why a man will not marry a pregnant woman if he doubts that he is the father. The Sebei do not talk about this underlying spiritual unity of the clan; they just assume it to be a natural condition of life. We saw this in Chapter 5 when Toboyi spoke with great fear against Kilele's performing *mumyantet*, from which he might die.

The social effect of this belief is clear. It makes every clansman support his kindred and it makes every man concerned with the behavior of his clansmen. Like it or not, a Sebei man is his brother's keeper. The spiritual and social importance of the clan would lead one to expect strong rituals to reinforce clan unity. This is not the case. Only two rituals involve the clan as such, and neither of them perform this role. One of them is a ritual of separation, a formal severance of ties initiated by a lineage that wants to dissociate itself from the other lineages of the clan and start a separate clan. The other is the ritual act of the removal of a curse. The curse to be removed may be either one that had been done against the clan or be one that a member of the clan had done against others and that, having done its work, is reflexively harming the clan of the perpetrator. We saw this ritual in an earlier chapter.

A Clan Meeting   The one meeting of clansmen that I had an opportunity to attend—they are rare events—was concerned with issues involving oaths and the harm the clan was suffering. Many instances of sickness and death had occurred and the clan wanted to discover their cause and plan necessary countermeasures. Both lineages of the clan were represented. Six separate matters were discussed.

1. An oath made by a mother in one of the lineages against the other lineage because of the murder of her children. A diviner had advised compensation, which the mother had refused before she died. The oathing substance had been transmitted to her daughter, who was now willing to have the ceremony for removal of the oath, but demanded compensation. A lengthy discussion followed on how to raise the money and beer.
2. A curse placed upon the Kapsamsama clan for the theft of a cow. No Kapsamsama representative was present, and nothing was decided "because it is they who are dying."
3. A curse placed on the meat of a stolen cow by its owner without warning his clansmen. It was made with a blocked arrow—the kind used for bleeding—

that was later hidden in a cave. This arrow was subsequently passed on to the owner's son. As both clans were losing members, the suggestion was made that no compensation be paid but that a ritual of amity be performed.

4. A curse by a married daughter of the clan who had been beaten to death. Before she died, she said, "If you kill me, let my blood live and kill all your family." Her father had re-evoked this curse at her grave. As this was internal to the clan and lineage, no compensation was needed but a *korosek* ceremony of oath removal was required.

5. A curse made by a man against his brother-in-law, who was keeping some of his cattle. The brother-in-law had used them for his brideprice but now claimed they had been stolen and should be replaced. The man cursed his brother-in-law, and members of his family were dying. As the principals in the original theft and curse had died, the clan feared that the curse would act reciprocally upon them. It was suggested that *korosek* be performed, with only a goat for compensation.

6. An oath against another clan for murder of one of its members, but this was dismissed since, "We are not the ones that are dying; let them come to us."

Consider the dominant mood of this meeting. First, it was a fearful mood; terrible things were happening and each person was afraid. Second, it was ridden with guilt and accusation. People had done wrong and evil acts needed to be atoned. Some of them were committed by clansmen and some by outsiders. Third, it was somber. No expression was made of the greatness of the clan, the privilege of being a member, nor were there expressions of pride in their past or anticipation of a better future. No such clan rituals exist among the Sebei. Clanship among the Sebei appears as a burden rather than a satisfaction.

TWINS AND OTHER SPECIAL CHILDREN

All other rituals of the Sebei deal with matters that are individual or that involve a small group. These include the classic rites of passage: a naming rite at birth, initiation, marriage, and death. They include a few ameliorative rites, of which *misisi/mukutanek* and friendship between half brothers are examples. Ritual acts also deal with anger and confrontation: oathing and the removal of oaths. Acts of witchcraft are also rituals expressing hostility. Divination of various kinds may also be called ritual acts. Finally, there are a number of rituals designed to meet conditions that are seen as particularly dangerous; the most important of these is the rite performed for the birth of twins.

In many societies the birth of twins is greeted with evidence of special awe, either feared or rejoiced at, depending upon local attitudes. Their birth often evokes special ceremonial activities. In the case of the Sebei, twins seem to be regarded with a certain degree of ambivalence.

Special Children   Before we examine the rites attending to them, we must look at the particular social status of persons who are called *tekeryontet*, special persons because of the circumstance of their births. A number of circumstances evoke special treatment: twins, a child born after twins have died, a child born after a number of previous children have died, and breech births. These children receive all kinds of special treatment throughout their lives in small ritual ways, ending with the fact that their bones are taken up after the flesh is gone and buried in special places. This is done for nobody else except the prophets.

The social role of the *tekeryontet* is enigmatic. He is viewed as particularly vulnerable to harm and must be protected by special amulets, medicines, and treatment; his spirit is weaker. His friends are warned not to hit him because it is bad for him to bleed. One told me, "Other children would tease me because I was wearing rings on my arms and legs, and some would try to pull them off off, but I was strict and didn't like them to break these things. I would wrestle with other children but not fight. I was specially treated by my parents. When I was annoyed, I would cry, and they would come to me, saying, 'Keep quiet, my *tekeryontet*.' When they spoke politely to me, mentioning that I was *tekeryontet*, I would become quiet, or if they asked me politely, I would do what they wanted. My father beat me only once, when I was grazing cattle and they destroyed somebody's crops. Before the circumcision, they came and shaved me, applied butter on my head, and spit beer on me."

A *tekeryontet* was traditionally not supposed to hunt or lead in warfare, but could engage in war. Enemies were not supposed to kill a *tekeryontet*, though the Kamamojong did not honor this rule. He or she is not to go into the house where beer is fermenting because it would spoil the beer. The most important fact about the male *tekeryontet* is that he participates in the leopard ceremony of the women rather than the lion ceremony of the men at the close of the initiation cycle.

Is it good to be a *tekeryontet*? One man said, "People like to be *tekeryontet* because whenever beer is to be brewed in the family of a *tekeryontet*, there must be extra beer, and when people start singing, they praise his name." Another said that the status was good because he was treated with special consideration and politeness. A non-*tekeryontet* said it was not good for a man "because you are despised and cannot join the lion ceremony."

Rites for Twins   The ritual demands on the parents of twins are costly, time consuming, and unpleasant. Yet it is a ceremony that continues to be assiduously performed. When twins are born, the mother is immediately confined to her house and cannot go out except to relieve herself or to sun herself where nobody can see her. She is under strict dietary taboos. Her husband may not see her or the infants or hear his wife's voice, and he must go about covered with a cloth as he is not to be seen. The mother's older children may visit her, but no man may enter her house and most women must stay away. The twins wear a twisted iron necklace, iron bracelets on each arm, and anklets and bells on their legs. They should have a necklace of cowrie shells strung on a rope made of black monkey fur, or at least one cowrie shell to ward off the evil eye.

The restrictions on the mother last until the ceremony is held, which may be delayed for weeks or even months as the husband must find a pregnant ewe for the rite, brew ample beer, find a willing ritualist, and meet other expenses. The ritualist must be a mother of twins who would herself have undergone the rite.

On the day of the ceremony the ritualist is greeted by the women of the host's clan with the sacred song of welcome, the same one as for initiates. She prepares the medicine over a special fire inside the house and cooks the medicine, compounded of diverse leaves, roots and bark, cow's milk, and beef. The pregnant ewe, concealed by skins, is brought into the house through a hole that has been cut into the wall and is greeted by the women in the same manner as the ritualist had been. The songs give thanks to the mother for bringing the blessing of twins; these songs also have lewd sexual references. The ewe is slaughtered by suffocation. The mother is given some of the amniotic fluid to drink with the medicine that was prepared and eats the grub of a dung beetle. While the animal is being skinned, the women sing and dance inside the house, accompanied on a zebra hide drum. The drum is beaten with the ewe's front hoof. The skin of the ewe is worn by the father during the ceremony. The husband and wife, hidden from the others and from each other, are garlanded with beads and vines; the father sometimes carries a similarly garlanded spear and also wears a cowbell over the shoulder.

A hole about two feet in diameter is dug about fifteen feet from where the hole was cut into the house. Some of the mud taken from this hole is mixed with chyme from the ewe's stomach and is used to anoint the mother, father, and ceremonialist. The hole outside is filled with water and the embryo taken from the ewe put into it. Two uncircumcised children, garlanded with vines, one with a special basket and the other with a shield and spear, climb on the roof of the house in which the mother had been confined. A circumcised clan sister of the father is given a shield and spear to hold.

The ritualist and the parents of the twins then emerge through the hole that was cut into the house and have chyme smeared on their heads and faces by women who have had twins. They then lead a procession that dances around the hole, the three principals in succession stepping into the hole and briefly dancing there. The two children on the roof carefully dance and this continues for some 15 minutes, with the parents dancing on the embryo at intervals several times. At the close, the assembled group dances around the woman's house; the two children on the roof are helped down and run about making charges and thrusts with their weapons, as if in a fight, feinting at those present. At the same time, another young woman carrying shield and spear dashes about pretending to spear people. The solemn mood is now broken and people greet the parents in the normal and appropriate manner. But they also insult them with remarks that would normally start a fight: "May devils circumcise you," "You are like tapeworms," "Eat feces," and so on. Those so minded may spit beer in blessing on the couple and are similarly blessed by each in return. The ceremony should conclude with beer and a feast.

This ritual is filled with symbolic expression, some widely used in Sebei

Photo 29. The parents of twins dancing on the embryo.

ritual and others unique to it. Among the elements that occur in other rituals are the act of seclusion that is found at initiation, funerals, and weddings, the use of chyme as a kind of purification, which is used at both initiations and funerals. Garlanding with vines is also a recurrent item. Other symbolic acts are unique: the slaughtering of a ewe and the use of her embryo is perhaps most clearly related to the issue of the rite—birth. But dancing on the roof and the mock-military implications of weapons and pretense at fighting has no such relevance. It is hard to find in these diverse symbolic acts a consistent message. Some of them, like the vines and the song of welcome, are essentially expressions of pleasure. The carrying of weapons and the mock fighting seem rather to be expressions of hostility, as do the ceremonially licensed insults at the close, though they are mixed with blessings of spewing beer. The couple who undergo the rite appear dour and unhappy, and dancing on the embryo, being smeared with the chyme and mud mixture and the consumption of amniotic fluid were expressly viewed as unpleasant by the participants.

Rituals are a means of communication; they transmit feeling rather than intellectual understanding. We have no difficulty in reading most of the symbolic expressions of the circumcision rites and can be fairly confident about what is going on sociologically and psychologically. But what are we to make of this ambiguous expression of sentiment?

Victor Turner, whose description of twin rituals among the Ndembu of central Africa is the most detailed analysis in modern times, has argued that the fundamental feelings attached to having twins is itself ambivalent. Indeed he entitles the chapter in his *The Ritual Process* that deals with the twin rites *"Paradoxes* of Twinship in Ndembu Ritual," (emphasis supplied) and relates this to the thesis that "the paradox that what is good (in theory) is bad (in practice) becomes the mobilizing point" of these rites. For the Ndembu, as for the Sebei, having children is a prime value, but caring for twins is a difficult burden. He points out that "twins are both good luck and reasonable fertility . . . and bad luck and excessive fertility."

The Sebei want children; they want to have descendants and increase the Sebei population. Yet this is not a joyous celebration. Furthermore, twins are not infrequently allowed to die of neglect. Men I knew were reluctant to undergo the rite. Yet the Sebei have not allowed the twin ritual to die out as they have so many of their other rituals. This suggests that its deeper meanings and implications still hold for the Sebei of today.

To say that the ambiguity of the symbolic expressions reflects the ambivalence the people have toward twins does not really explain the ritual. But it is, frankly, the only explanation that Turner or I can offer. Why then describe the ritual? First, because it remains an intensely felt and dramatic aspect of Sebei life and through it we learn something about how the Sebei behave, whether or not we understand why. Second, because it is important to recognize that the life patterns of a people contain many puzzling elements. None of us has all the answers.

RITES OF PASSAGE

We have already witnessed the major rites of passage: initiations, weddings, and funerals. These rituals all require a period of seclusion for the person on whom the rite focuses and whose status is being transformed: the initiates themselves, the bride whose affiliation and residence is changed, and the widow who will become another man's wife. They are seen as being particularly vulnerable to the dangers of the world—"like a sick person," the Sebei say. But they are also dangerous, their aura can bring disaster to those around them. They must therefore behave in ways that will both protect them from harm and prevent them from bringing harm to others.

These rites seem to be grim and laden with presentiments of danger. Rarely is there any evidence of joy or expression of pleasure in human mutuality. One would not expect this at funerals—though it does happen elsewhere—but even these are made more ominous by their legal involvements. But one might expect them at initiations and at weddings as well as at the rite for twins, which in its form if not its function belongs to the same class as the other three rites. There were only two points in the whole initiation cycle when there was evidence of gaiety: the trick or treat evening and, very briefly, in dancing after the initiates were released. The only time I saw evidence of a sense of pleasure in social cohesion was at the final ceremony of the women, and here it took the form of antagonism toward outsiders, particulary toward men. Marriage rites are so suffused with confrontation, both between husband and wife and between their respective lineages, that any feeling of pleasure that might occur seems to have been squeezed out.

DOMESTIC RITES

Another class of rituals may be designated domestic rites. These consist of a number of rituals surrounding minor social realignments. Some relate to the establishment of a new relationship. For instance, when a child is born to a widow who has been inherited, the couple will have a special ritual involving the slaughter of a ram or ox during which the chyme is smeared on them and on their children. When a widower remarries and his new wife becomes pregnant, a ram is slaughtered. The stones are removed from the hearth and the chyme put around the fireplace before the stones are returned. A person who has himself undergone the ceremony earlier blesses the husband and wife with beer. The ceremony is performed so that the spirit of the deceased wife will do no harm to the child.

Cattle Inheritance Ritual   A more elaborate rite is held to unite cattle that are inherited (along with an inherited wife) with the existing herd. The man who inherits a herd must build a new *kraal*. An arch is formed over the gate with bamboo from the forest and a palm frond implanted at opposite ends, tied together at the top with a vine. The ritual is presided over by a man who has previously inherited a herd. A large fire is lit in the middle of the *kraal* and as guests arrive they throw healing *korosek* plants and the fat and chyme from a slaughtered ram into it.

All line up outside the *kraal* in the following order: the ritualist, his real wives, the widows he has inherited, the inheritor, his own wives and their children in the order of their marriage and age, then each inherited widow and her children in the order of marriage and age, followed by the herd of the owner and the herd he is inheriting. The procession goes into the *kraal* and the ceremonial leader strikes together an ax blade and a pick, circles the fire and goes back out, then circles about and reenters the *kraal*, making the circut four times. The people in the procession then enter the house of the senior wife and partake of milk taken from cows in each herd, to which fat from the ram's tail and beer are added. The ritual has similarities to that for amity between half-brothers. There are also rituals to be performed when a woman has had sexual intercourse with another man, because "it is dangerous for the semen of two men to be mixed." Clearly this whole group of rites are designed to establish a spirit of amity where tension is apt to prevail because of jealousy—sometimes, as explicitly stated, the jealousy of the deceased.

Rites for Children   Other domestic rites concern children. The spiritual name of a child is determined by divination on the fourth day after birth. An awl is stuck in the floor of the house and encircled with a ring of beer or milk. A hard, round, hollow pod is filled with water and balanced on the handle while the names of deceased relatives of the infant are called out successively. If the pod fails to balance, it is because another spirit has knocked it off. When the pod balances on the handle four successive times, the child is given that relative's name because the spirit wishes to have the child named after him or her. It is said that the spirits frequently quarrel over this privilege and if the pod does not balance it is assumed that many spirits are seeking the child, and he or she is given the name Kiteyo, "many spirits."

There are also ceremonies for children whose canines or molars erupt before the incisors, for this is considered the result of evil spirits that must be removed.

A number of domestic rites have to do with cattle, in addition to the one just described. An animal may be dedicated to spirits that are thought to be causing the illness of a family member. There is a special ritual for establishing the bull of the herd and another performed when he dies. The allocation of animals to wives is also done ritually.

Agricultural Rites   Very few rites have to do with agriculture. *Misisi* certainly was one, as was the plantain ritual that was borrowed from the Bantu people. Two other agricultural rites were described to me but I never witnessed them. One is for a kind of first-fruit ceremony opening a new plantain *shamba*. Before any plantains have been harvested, the owner slaughters a ram and builds a fire in the garden. A bit of the chyme from the ram is thrown at each shoot, and the word *anyin* (sweet) is repeated. The people present bring cleansing plants to throw on the fire. Some of the plantains are then harvested and cooked, and this and the ram are eaten.

Another ritual, also a kind of first-fruit ceremony, is performed to placate the spirits. As each woman cooks the first of each crop to be harvested, she gives her husband some of the food to scatter—first to the good spirits with his right hand inside the house and then to the bad spirits with his left hand away from the house. The food should be boiled with ram's tail fat and chyme. This ceremony was not done for maize—"that is too recent." Here again is a situation that one might expect to call forth expressions of delight and thanksgiving, but in fact expresses the placation of potentially hostile spirits.

OATHING AND WITCHCRAFT

The last ritual behaviors we will examine are those specifically designed to harm others. We have already seen these in action and know that both oathing and witchcraft harness supernatural forces and differ chiefly in their social meaning—one being legal and the other not.

Oaths   In ordinary Sebei discourse, there is frequent reference to both oaths and witchcraft. Sebei will, when angry, accuse one another by insinuation or direct statement of having performed black magic and will as readily assert their willingness to take an oath of innocence. Such expressions are generally not taken seriously but are treated more like our use of expletives. Curses are not seriously regarded if only words are used. They escalate to more serious challenges if the curse evokes some sacred object such as the skin that the man stood on while being circumcised or his mother's cowrie shell girdle. This is rather like swearing on a Bible.

But a curse really becomes serious when some substance is used. As in cases we have already referred to, such substance may be parts of the person, animal, or other thing that is the object of the quarrel. They may involve the creation of special substances, such as urinating in a gourd or killing a dog in a ritual manner. There may also be more public oaths around a special altar involving the whole clan, though these have long since disappeared—or perhaps really have become clouded in secrecy.

Witchcraft   Again, the line between oath and witchcraft is a fine one; it is not so much in the understanding of how it works or even in the kind of action taken as it is in the perceived legitimacy of the act. If a man suffers damage he may legitimately make an oath as a means of retaliation. These oaths generally only work on a person who is guilty—or on his clansmen. But if a man, out of hatred or anger, performs magic against another without just cause, this is witchcraft and is illegal. Sebei do not generally admit to witchcraft. This is particularly true of such witchcraft as may cause illness, disaster, or death. There are more domestic forms of witchcraft also. Chief among these are the kind that women perform against men. A barren woman will suspect witchcraft as the cause and most frequently blame a co-wife. Magical means are known for making an initiate cry the knife, as we have seen.

THE GENERAL CHARACTER OF SEBEI RELIGION

Generalizations about Sebei religion cover three dimensions: historical, sociological, and psychological. The historical dimension is important for the Sebei because they underwent such drastic changes. The basic elements of Sebei religion derive from its pastoralist past. This is demonstrated by the symbolic elements in their rituals: livestock, their products and their parts, the spear and shield, many wild plants that are associated with both good and evil purposes, and *kraals* represented in miniature and as the location for rites. Cultivated plants play a minor role, even in the harvest *korosek*. The ritual for a new plantain *shamba* requires the slaughter of a ram and the use of chyme. There is no garden magic nor are there any garden shrines. Clearly, religious activity did not make the transition to the farming way of life.

The second historic element has to do with the abandonment of much religious practice. All the national rites were entirely abandoned by the mid-1920s at the latest; that is, within less than a quarter of a century after the Baganda subjugated the territory. The one apparent exception, circumcision, lost its national character and has become a local, if not actually domestic, rite. There are two possible reasons for this rapid decline. Outlawing the prophets (the major one was incarcerated by the British for his alleged sedition) took away the coordinator's role. But a deeper reason may be that a sufficiently strong sense of involvement with locality to preserve the need for such rites never developed.

This leads us to the sociological side of religious belief and performance. The sociological purpose of religion is to reinforce each individual's commitment to his or her social role, and more important, the individual's sense of belonging to a social group. We should realize, however, that pastoralism is a form of economy that places great importance on the essential *independence of the individual*, because individuals must often act alone in their herding activities. The personal character of property rights in livestock reinforces this individualism. Despite this emphasis, group commitment is still essential. Three kinds of social groups toward which such commitment should be felt by Sebei are the age set, the clan, and the *pororyet*.

The strongest group reinforcement through ritual occurred with the age set. Furthermore, the rites that gave strength to this group also focused upon the individual in his advancement, so that this rite has been retained at full strength despite the changes that have occurred. However, the functional usefulness of the age set was undermined by the economic transition of the Sebei as they adapted to the mountain environment. Hence this rite no longer has the function of group reinforcement to any significant degree.

Clan unity was essential for mutual support in Sebei internal conflicts; it is the ultimate protection against murder and theft. It receives deep-seated support in the ideology of oathing. But there is no evidence that it receives any support in ritual life. We saw that the only clan rites performed are intended to eliminate danger. None of them express the joys and satisfaction of clan membership, and it appears that there are none. We saw in the matter of Kambuya's heritage that brotherhood, which necessarily is also clan brotherhood, was suffused with rivalry and hatred. When the elders moralized on the conduct of Kambuya's sons, they argued for amity among them and the need to accept the leadership of Salimu as the senior, but they did not at any time evoke the image of clan unity and, so far as I know, never mentioned clanship at all. Nowhere did I ever hear that there had been positive clan rites in the past, though in songs there are often ennobling references to the clan. The absence of ritual reinforcements for this essential institution is puzzling. Perhaps the importance of the clan was so much an accepted fact that it did not require any ritual support.

My historical reconstruction suggests that the *pororyet* became an important element in the structure of Sebei society as a result of the increased importance of location that derived from their shift to agricultural pursuits. There were ritual supports to the *pororyet* in the *korosek* rites, as well as in the fact that any individual who wanted to join a *pororyet* had to do so by a public ritual. But these rites are surprisingly negative. Nothing in them was designed to ennoble citizenship or extol the virtues of the locale. They are "fat" ceremonies, in the Sebei expression, but they are not joyous gatherings. The harvest *korosek* might be expected to be a positive expression of community solidarity, a song to the bounty nature has provided. However, the Sebei see it as ritual purification designed to counteract disease, drought, and bad luck. The other *pororyet* ritual, *chomi ntarastit*, utilizes the dread oath as a means of providing social solidarity. Much as I admire the invention of this rite as a device to give legitimacy to the local community to police its membership, it was certainly built on fear and hostility rather than on loyalty and devotion. We may reasonably ask whether the ineffectiveness of Sebei military performance was not impaired by this failure of esprit.

The psychological side of religious expression has two facets. The first is the overt expression of feeling, the ordering of public sentiment. The second is the underlying psychology of the people, the ethos. The former can be illustrated by a few examples. The manifest purpose of an oathing is to express overt hostility (whereas witchcraft expresses covert hostility). Clearly the function of initiation is to shift the attitudes of the initiate to those of an adult and the attitudes of others toward him or her to recognize this adult status. Likewise the wedding transfers the bride from the context of her natal family to that of her husband's. Or again, the feeling of amity between in-laws that *misisi* was designed to create was transformed to allay new sources of conflict by the reformulation to *mukutanek*.

Consider the ritual for half-brothers at which Psiwa officiated; it is aimed directly at the potential rivalry between the sons of a man by different wives. There is some evidence in the form of the ceremony that it is an adaptation of a presumably older rite of blood brotherhood, the creation of a bond between two men who like each other very much and establish brotherhood by proclamation. But the psychology has been transformed, for now it *demands*, rather than expresses, friendship where hostility is expected.

SEBEI ETHOS

But of more interest is the evidence of the psychology of the Sebei: the Sebei ethos. When we look beneath the surface of Sebei ritual behavior, we sense that the Sebei see the world as essentially hostile, that they are an anxious people suffused with fear and suspicion. Most of their domestic rituals are built on the assumption of animosity—even among the cattle. The *oyik* are never appealed to for help; even the good spirits are only requested to do no harm.

Anxiety   This fearfulness is diffuse rather than specific. The world is not filled with ogres that have a specified form or a particular location. The model for this attitude is best seen in the harvest *korosek*, which is designed to rid the *pororyet* of unspecified illness. If the slopes of Mount Elgon were disease infested, if the Sebei lived in a malarial swampland, such notions might have a realistic quality. But they live in a physically lovely and benign land. The major danger to life is the constant threat of warfare with more violent tribes. Their rituals do not face this reality. The real threat that Sebei rituals deal with is their own hostility.

Robert Edgerton found this endemic hostility in the psychological tests he performed. His study embraced the four tribes of our Culture and Ecology Project and he therefore can contrast the Sebei to others. Two attitudinal characteristics of the Sebei are directly relevant: hostility and diffuse anxiety. Of the former he says:

> Of all the tribes, the Sebei rank lowest on cooperation. Their profound jealousy is not confined to wealthy men: "We are jealous of everyone!" And, "Everyone hates me—my clan, everyone." Or, this: "Perhaps my friends may plot to kill me. Who will protect me?" Or this . . . "We Sebei always backbite; we talk against everyone."

On diffuse anxiety, he wrote:

> "The Sebei are fearful, not merely of specific dangers, but of everything: 'We are afraid of everything,' or, 'We Sebei are cowards, we are afraid even to fight. We are all afraid.' " Among the four tribes, only the Sebei regularly commented that the two men who face each other in threatening posture [shown in one of the picture tests used] are afraid to fight: "They are afraid—they will not fight"; or again, "They are bluffing, they are trying to win without fighting." Similarly, there is great concern with protection against vague dangers—with dogs to warn of sounds in the night, with friends to protect one against one's clan, with clansmen to protect one against one's friends, with luck to protect one against everything. Even where adultery is concerned, the Sebei are anxious. For example, members of all four tribes expressed some fear lest they be caught in the act of adultery, but only the Sebei responded to the picture of the man and woman [a values picture showing a man and woman seated on a cot] as follows: "He is saying, 'Let us do it quickly before someone comes and finds us.' " In the Rorschach and throughout the response protocol, the Sebei made more anxious remarks than did members of any other tribe.

Fear of Death   A third characteristic that emerged in these tests was a fear of death, an attitude that Edgerton characterizes as a "fearful dread" and goes on to say: "It is not the means of death that the Sebei fear: disease, violence, and witchcraft are equally to be feared." Remember the funeral of Seswet, where the rituals were directed neither at the body nor the soul of Seswet, but at death itself.

These negative forces are not particularized; the emphasis is not on the evil of witches or other individual representations, nor on particular situations out of which danger arises, nor is it related to breaches of taboo or the commission of sins, though such may also bring disaster and are in the ambience within which the Sebei dwell. The Sebei are anxious about life, not fearful of things.

Why this fearfulness? Why the negativism in religious expression? The two are certainly related, but we cannot say that one causes the other. I believe both emerge out of the disruption that stems from social change. We will examine this in the concluding chapter.

8 / The process of adaptation

AN OVERVIEW OF THE CHANGE PROCESS

Cultures are always undergoing change. Sometimes change is so slow that it is barely perceptible. Sometimes it is rapid, as has been the case with the Sebei. We are now ready to look at the process of change, that is, to review the information on the Sebei in terms of the dynamics of cultural adaptation.

We will look at this process from two angles: historical development and regional variation. The former is like the paleontological record showing variation. The latter is like comparative anatomy, showing diversity. The two kinds of information complement one another, for the historical data show big changes but lack the intimate details, whereas the comparative data give these details without the massive differences. Together these show the process at work.

The Individual as Change Agent   We can draw another analogy to biological evolution. The changes in time and the differences between varieties in biological evolution begin with changes that take place in the individual. In biology, of course, this occurs through mutation in the genes, which alter in some form the potential for behavior that, when beneficial, are selected for and ultimately create a population of a different character. Culture change also has its basis in the individual, not in inheritance but in individual perceptions, attitudes, and actions. Under stable conditions, variations in these individual qualities will have little effect on the population as a whole. But when circumstances are changed, then new forms of behavior can prove effective and will be selected for.

The process of change involves a sequence of three events: choice of action, institutionalization, and unanticipated consequences. This sets up a cycle of activities as the consequences call forth new choices of action.

People are always choosing a course of action; culture is never a rigid prescription. When new circumstances arise, noncustomary forms of behavior may prove more satisfying, and many people will do things that are previously deviant or unheard of behavior. Choice is not always the right word, however, because it implies a conscious measurement of alternatives and rational

129

selection. Sometimes these alternate forms are sentiments that arise without an act of will, as we will see, and these may also influence action.

Institutionalization   When a number of people have taken a new course of action, it becomes regularized and the behavior appropriate to it is seen as customary; the new situation is thus institutionalized. This can happen either when the new behavior is seen as a legitimate alternative or when it has become the norm. (I can best illustrate this with an example taken from another people, the Hupa Indians of California whose culture I studied in 1937. At their major annual ritual, several rivalrous leaders each provide a feast for the guests. One of them had for the first time that year set up a picnic table, but the others gossiped about this, saying that it was improper, or even sacrilegious. When I recently visited the Hupa, each group had tables for their guests and denied ever having thought it wrong to do so.)

Secondary Consequences   The new situation will have consequences for social behavior that were not foreseen. Consider, for instance, all the un-anticipated consequences of the fact that people chose to have automobiles: the corporate structures, the network of roads, the new mobility and even, some believe, changes in sexual mores. These consequences become the motivation for further change.

PREHISTORIC ADAPTATION

The arrival on Mount Elgon and the knowledge of corn and plantain cultivation offered to the Sebei new opportunities for behavior. It is easy to picture the Sebei increasingly diverting attention to their farming enterprises and giving less to their livestock. Concern with farming made it convenient, if not necessary, to live near their *shambas* to protect the crops from marauding animals and theft. This process probably began in the wetter western section and spread to the east, but it was completed before the Europeans arrived.

Structural Changes   As people moved on to the land it became necessary to set up new institutional arrangements to deal with the new social situation. For one thing, it had the unanticipated consequence of abandoning the old *manyatta* organization, which had been structured in terms of age sets. Social units based on geography were needed to organize people who were now neighbors. Thus they formed the villages and *pororyets*. Each of these had places set aside where village and *poroyet* affairs could be discussed, where men could hammer out amicable settlements of disputes. Though they never created formal offices, they did recognize some outstanding men with wisdom who could act as judges—though they were judges without power to enforce their decisions.

These geographical units had to protect themselves from outsiders. Warfare was no longer waged through cattle raiding, but became defensive. This meant that it was necessary to reorganize the conduct of war, for it became the responsibility of all able-bodied men to serve in the defense of country. The unit of defense became the *pororyet*. Since a military unit must know friend from enemy, *pororyet* membership had to be formalized. Therefore, a man who wished to change his *pororyet* affiliation had to give two feasts, one for the men of the *pororyet* he left and another for the *pororyet* he entered.

Other rituals strengthened *pororyet* ties; indeed, all the important community rites were organized by *pororyets*—even the circumcision rituals. *Pororyet* interdependence was expressed by the coordination of these rites by the prophets and their performance in orderly sequence.

Another institution developed in that part of Mount Elgon formerly occupied by Sebei but lost to the Gisu: political function of the clans. All we know about it is that these Sebei fought their wars as clan units—which other Sebei never did—and settled into clan villages when they retreated to the east and joined other Sebei. This suggests that the clan had become the institutionalized basis for much social activity. This system was abandoned, leaving only a few villages with populations dominated by specific clans and named after them.

Authority These developments undermined the role of the age set, once the basis for *manyatta* organization, the unit of military operations, and an institution for control and at least informal authority. The age-set loss of both function and structure was an unanticipated consequence of more basic change. Because initiation rites were so very important for the individual, the age set continued, but became an essentially hollow institution, serving social rather than political functions.

This loss of the age set's political function left a power vacuum. Conflict always had the potential for escalating into a feud, but as long as the clans were more or less equal in strength and as long as the oath was an effective instrument for controlling the unbridled use of power, peaceful relationships could be maintained by age-structured authority. Under pastoral conditions, furthermore, a man could depart with his family and stock when he found conditions unbearable. Such departure became almost impossible for farmers, who would have to abandon their property if they left. The prophet Matui tried to remedy this power vacuum by creating *chomi ntarastit*—an oath taken by all men of the *pororyet* that they would not commit any of a list of crimes. This oath gave the community the right to punish acts of crime—a legal principle that did not formerly exist.

Land Ownership The move to farming transformed land from an essentially public good into private property. This, too, can be seen as an unanticipated consequence. There always had been some farming, and it had always been the rule that when bush was cleared for a *shamba*, the land belonged to those who had done the work, so long as they continued to use it. But under early conditions these *shambas* lost their fertility after two or three years and were allowed to return to bush, and private landholding was unimportant. However, nearly all the land came to be privately held as agriculture increased, especially with the cultivation of plantains, which were permanently productive. The traditional rules of property rights that applied to livestock came to be applied to land. This undoubtedly worked well enough as long as enough was available to all, but when land became scarce (as it was ultimately bound to) it worked very poorly and led to a good deal of conflict, both within and between families.

This heightened conflict between neighbors led to the transformation of *misisi* to *mukutanek*. This small domestic ritual was designed to reaffirm friendship between such neighbors and alleviate the irritation they felt toward one another. It is an example of the adjustment of an existing institution to a new condition. This change is intriguing because, while one can understand *why* it took place, it is hard to understand *how* it took place. After all, there was no resident sociologists to suggest the reorientation, and the stress between in-laws did not disappear. It shows, however, that institutions are responsive to the emotional tensions that a social order creates.

The development of agriculture led to changes in the household operations. Though we cannot know much about the ancient household, we do know that men married very late and that the family units were an integrated part of *manyatta* camp life. The adaptation to horticulture took the household out of the camp and made of it a more nearly independent unit. Because men had no cattle to tend, they married earlier. Indeed, traditionalist Sebei told in shocked tones that the men in the intensive horticultural area actually married before they were circumcised. (Tradition held that it was dirty to have sexual intercourse with an unmarried man.) This difference disappeared when circumcision was performed on men at an earlier age. Since the men were not away at cattle camps or raids, they were inevitably more a part of the household than they had been in earlier years.

These chains of events significantly altered the fabric of Sebei life. They changed the nature of the daily routine of individuals; they reoriented the significant social context of these events; they reformulated the social units that called forth personal loyalties; and they realigned authority. These changes were in process, having gone further in some parts of Sebei than in others, when the Europeans arrived and brought a new set of conditions. Because the Sebei had also to adjust to these, we must examine them before looking at the comparative data.

THE PROCESS OF HISTORIC CHANGE

What major changes were brought about by the British and the establishment of the Uganda Protectorate? Even before Europeans came, Swahili caravans had arrived, trading beads and other manufactured goods for ivory, cattle, and foodstuff. The first European visited Sebei in 1890; a supply base was established to provide food for military operations in the Sudan in 1898. About five years later, a general of the Buganda army invaded the territory and established governmental control. British authority arrived around 1910. They relinquished that authority in 1962, when the Protectorate became the independent nation of Uganda. The imposition of external rule and the introduction of alien goods, concepts, and organizational principles affected every aspect of Sebei life either directly or indirectly. Here we can discuss only the major influences.

Before we turn to these influences, we must recognize that change imposed from the outside is different in an important way from the ecological adaptations already described. These adaptations were made because the people perceived a new situation and adjusted their life to it. We may think of this as *natural adaptation*. While even such change creates difficulties, it is essentially rooted in practical conditions. Changes introduced by conquerors, however benign in intent, are not rooted in local practical conditions. Basically, conquest brings about changes that are imposed in the interest of the conquerors. It may be thought of as *forced change* that establishes a new context for behavior. Yet within that context, the subject people make their own adaptations.

The British destroyed or severely curtailed some traditional institutions. The most important of these was the banning of the prophets, who played a role in unifying the Sebei as a people and in setting up the community-oriented rituals. All of these rituals disappeared very quickly and reduced the strength of the *pororyet*. They also established the military garrisons, prevented major wars, and reduced cattle raiding. This also diminished the importance of the *pororyet*, as well as other institutions of local control. The British also outlawed the use of witchcraft and oathing, and this undermined the legitimate instruments for legal decision making.

The British replaced these traditional institutions with a bureaucratic hierarchy—districts, subdistricts, and lesser units, each with its appointed chiefs and other officers— which also served as a court system. This system was based on one that existed in Buganda. One aspect of these courts was the reliance on witnesses rather than oaths, which the Sebei consider to be far less reliable. This took away the major function of the clan, which previously was responsible for adjucating disputes and whose ultimate authority came from the dreadful power of the oaths.

The government also introduced the use of money and established a system of markets. It imposed head taxes, so that every man had to earn at least some money—even if only by working as a common laborer on the roads and other public works. This involved the Sebei in the international economy —so much so that already by the 1930s they could feel the effects of the Great Depression in the lowered price of cattle. Aside from the sale of livestock, cash crops (cotton on the plains, which proved unsuccessful, and coffee on the mountain) offered a source of money and gave some Sebei men an active interest in agriculture.

A wide range of consumer goods was made available and made it important to have money. These ranged from such everyday items as sugar, tea, soap, and kerosene, which rapidly became essentials, to prestige items such as clothes, bicycles, and, in later years, cars for the most affluent.

Missionaries—Catholic, Anglican, and Moslem—brought schools for the children as well as a variety of different ways of looking at the world. This had the effect of diversifying beliefs, undermining traditional religious convictions, and lessening involvement with ancient rites. The missions, as well as the government, also provided modern medicines and medical dispensaries.

Finally, the Europeans introduced firearms and the knowledge of converting native beer into a powerful gin. The guns were strictly controlled and had little effect on the Sebei during the colonial era, but the liquor transformed social drinking into problem drinking.

These changes took place throughout Sebeiland; indeed, they have taken place throughout the colonial world. They heavily influenced the context within which Sebei lived. But within that context, the Sebei established their own detailed patterns of living. Adjustments took place in essentially the same way that they had taken place in the prehistoric adptations. That is, they started with choices made by individuals, the institutionalization of new practices, and unanticipated consequences of these developments. The Sebei adjusted their way of life differently in different parts of their country because local ecological conditions varied. Such local adjustments were matters of indifference to the government. It is to these different patterns of life that we now turn, for they show the more intimate aspects of cultural adaptation. The plains/mountain differences in many ways parallel the historical difference so that some of the same issues will arise.

ECOLOGICAL ADAPTATIONS

Sasur and Kapsirika represent for us the life patterns of the Sebei under intense horticulture and maximal pastoral pursuits, respectively. We used the communities as statistical units and as a base for the observation of ongoing social behavior. Our observations are not limited to these communities, and our comparison applies to the differences in regional life modes rather than the villages themselves.

Kapsirika is *not* old Sebei, encapsulated. It was settled by men who had already adapted to the mountain environment—though few if any had come from the plantain area—and had lived for 10 or more years under colonial domination. Immigrants to the plains probably retained more traditional elements than the people of Sasur, but that is not the real difference. They readapted their life to the plains conditions. Thus, in Nyelit, the neighboring village to Kapsirika, the people established an enclosed *manyatta*. This looks like ancient Sebei behavior, but it was not sociologically the same. The traditional *manyatta* was strictly organized according to age sets and had other structural features. These were not created in Nyelit, where the people simply settled close to one another and enclosed the area with a brush fence, without formal social structure. The *idea* of an enclosure undoubtedly came from remembered tradition, the *impulse* to create it came from the same kind of environmental hazards, but the *form* was different.

Environmental Differences   The underlying difference between Sasur and Kapsirika—between the western part of the escarpment and the plains—is the environment itself. Sasur has high rainfall (over 70 inches per year) and steeply sloped contours; Kapsirika is semiarid (less than 30 inches of rain per year), flat and covered with bush and grass. Sasur is ideally suited to hoe cultivation but not to plow agriculture or cattle keeping; Kapsirika is ideally suited to livestock and poorly suited to hoe cultivation, though it is amenable to more extensive plow agriculture. Also, the plains are vulnerable to raiding, since the land is flat and close to the borders of the intensely cattle-keeping areas of the Karamojong and Pokot, who continue to steal cattle. Sasur is protected from such aggression, especially under colonial rule.

These environmental differences made it necessary for the people in the two areas to take different courses of action. In Sasur, they took up the cultivation of plantains and later the production of coffee, making the land permanently useful and highly valuable. In Kapsirika, the men increased their livestock and devoted major effort to animal husbandry, though they supplemented this with the cultivation of fields of grain prepared with ox-drawn plows.

In Sasur, intensive cultivation meant that the people were tightly packed on the land in permanent dwellings. Each home was usually within earshot of others. The Kapsirika economy demanded that the people scatter over the land, so that a house might be a half mile from the nearest neighbor. Land had little value, the houses were less well constructed, and people were free to move their residence. Indeed, many men had lived in different villages in the plains. Under these conditions, relationships among neighbors raised few problems and if problems did arise, it was easy for one or the other simply to move away.

On the other hand, the plains offered different kinds of hazards. Animals are vulnerable to attack from the wild animals, and the herdsmen had to be alert to these dangers. More importantly, the Pokot to the east and the Karamojong to the north continued to engage in cattle raiding, despite the presence of police, and this posed a threat to both life and property. Kapsirika men had to be prepared to face these dangers, which were unknown in Sasur.

The different choices of productive activity were inevitable, and the immediate consequences with respect to settlement pattern and work roles were essentially unavoidable. How did these differences affect the social behavior in the two communities? To answer that question we will have to look at the quality of the careers that men and women have in the two communities. Anthropologists do not often look at individual careers, but I think that they are a major key to understanding social institutions.

Careers   A career is the series of activities a person engages in through the course of his or her life to achieve personal satisfaction. The central activity is productivity—the things the person does to gain a livelihood and contribute to the general welfare of the community. But career satisfactions are more than merely getting food and other goods; they are the achievement of personal standing and social recognition. Having and rearing children, demonstrating competences, and appropriate comportment and lifestyle are also parts of career activities.

Careers are defined differently in different cultures for two reasons. First, the kinds of work essential to gaining a livelihood differs. This is explicitly the case with respect to Sasur and Kapsirika. Second, the situations and conditions that people define as satisfactions differ. That is another way of saying that cultural values differ. These also vary between Sasur and Kapsirika. In speaking of careers, we are concerned both with the means by which satisfactions are achieved and with what is seen as giving satisfaction.

We must recognize one other feature of the idea of career. Individual careers vary in quality within each culture. Some people get more satisfaction and some less. That is to say, some people are more successful than others. The people themselves are aware of this and make judgments about others—and about themselves—with respect to these matters. Persons who see themselves as deprived are often personally distressed, and such distress it apt to lead to actions designed to alleviate the situation. A person who feels, rightly or not, that somebody is hampering his own development is likely to feel hostility. Such situations often lead to witchcraft or the accusation of witchcraft.

The careers of the men and women in Sasur differ from those in Kapsirika, and it is the pursuit of these different kinds of careers that lies at the heart of the differences between the two communities. Let us first consider the careers of Kapsirika men. A Kapsirika man achieves success by building up a large herd of cattle. To do this, he must display a number of talents. First, he must know how to take care of animals—know how to herd, how to evaluate the quality of grass, recognize when animals are ill and need treatment, and the like. This can be summarized by saying that he must be sensitive to the needs of his stock. He begins his apprenticeship early by tending sheep, goats, and calves. Second, he must acquire animals. Most boys start by demanding gifts of animals from their relatives. These demands are usually made during ceremonies, especially when his incisors are removed and during circumcision. He must display bravery, self-control, and even a measure of bravado. Third, he must be prepared to protect his animals from raiders. Going on offensive raids against neighboring tribes is also good, but the Sebei rarely do so nowadays. He must also have the courage to protect the stock from wild animals—lions, leopards, and hyenas. Fourth, he must be shrewd in the sale, purchase, and exchange of animals. This involves a number of talents: knowing whom to trust, being able to judge the condition of livestock, and knowing how to engage in fair but advantageous bargaining. These abilities require subtle social skills. A man must also recognize that he needs the help and support of others and so must use his cattle—the only tangible asset he has—to forge alliances, cement friendships, and create a following.

The careers of Sasur men are not so easily defined. The successful men are those who have much land, and a few men were building up their holdings, as we have seen with Psiwa and his sons. Few men can do this unless they had inherited land to begin with. The acquisition of land is different from building up a herd because Sebei men do not work the land; women transform land into goods. This deprives the men of the satisfaction of endeavor and renders their daily lives relatively meaningless. Furthermore, only a few men can really engage in this pursuit since land is limited and one man's gain means another man's loss, which is not the case with cattle. The men who engage in land transactions are essentially antagonists, in contrast to those who make cattle contracts, which create social bonds. There is the further difference that the expectations and training of childhood do not lead to the performance requirements of adult life in Sasur.

Because Sasur men do not have as much satisfaction from their opportunities, they are more likely to choose a career that draws them into the modern world—entering public service through the hierarchy of chiefs or as teachers. Less frequently, they open shops or become traders.

Such a career requires education—in the earlier days, merely literacy, nowadays, a secondary education. These activities bring men into closer involvement with Western patterns of living, and they find themselves having to compromise between imported and native values. I remember talking to one young political leader who was trying to decide whether to take a fourth wife or spend his money on school fees for his oldest son.

Sasur women, on the other hand, have more satisfactory careers then their sisters in Kapsirika—or so it seems to me. Women from the Sasur area of intensive cultivation do not want to move to the plains, for they feel life there is more difficult. They work hard, but their work provides the material well-being of their household and gives them the satisfaction of performance. If they are provided adequate land by their husbands, they can be part of a community of women who, through participation in *moykets*, enjoy a network of social relationships.

Kapsirika women gain their social status chiefly from having sons become successful pastoralists and take many wives. This is the traditional basis for self-evaluation of Sebei women. To achieve such success she must induce her husband to allocate cows to her—animals with which she will feed her children and which will be for the brideprice of her sons. Since she has a say in the daily handling of the cattle given to her and in any transaction made with them, her knowledge and her skill in getting her voice heard affects the success she will achieve, though much still depends on her husband's capabilities.

Kapsirika women have *moykets*, but these are relatively rare. Women spend a greater portion of time among their co-wives than with other women in the community. They seem lonely. Their lives are physically difficult. This is shown by their low fertility rate. They bear 20 percent fewer children than the women in Sasur; over half of their children die, as against 29 percent in Sasur. They show more evidence of depression than the people of Sasur.

INSTITUTIONAL DIVERSITY

The circumstances described above shape the institutional patterns in the two communities to the requirements of each. Most of the differences are modifications of traditional practice, though a few are essentially new institutions.

Marriage   Marriage patterns differ. Most Sebei men want to marry; most would like to have several wives. "A man with one wife," a Sebei proverb goes, "is neighbor to a bachelor," for if she becomes ill or incapacitated he must undertake the irksome household chores that Sebei men disdain.

In both communities men continue to make a payment to the father of the bride for the privilege of marrying his daughter. The payment is substantially lower in Sasur than in Kapsirika: an average of 5 cows as against 6.6; 15 percent less total value of goods is transferred. They also have a greater out-standing debt on what they had agreed to pay (34 percent as against 18 percent). Nevertheless, it is more difficult for Sasur men to marry, because they have fewer cattle and, more important, because they need to have land for their wives to cultivate. This difficulty is reflected in fewer polygamous marriages. In Sasur only ten men (17 percent) were living with more than one wife, two of whom had three wives, while in Kapsirika, sixteen men (37 percent) were living with more than one wife, eight of whom had three. Furthermore, the Sasur men who had more than one wife waited, on the average, two years longer to marry the later ones.

Each wife must be given her own *shambas* to work. This is not a problem in Kapsirika, for there is no shortage of land. Kapsirika men handle the ox-drawn plows, and they are always careful to prepare the same amount of land for each wife to avoid creating jealousy among them. In Sasur, each wife is always given land, but it is by no means so easy to be equitable, and jealousies and conflicts occur between co-wives, as we saw in Chapters 4 and 5. The increasing difficulty of supplying wives with land is shown by the fact that older men have more *shambas* to provide their wives than do the younger men. The average age of the men whose wives cultivated more than ten *shambas* each was 47 years; the average age of those whose wives have only three or four *shambas* was 30 years.

Households   Sasur households more often consist of a man, wife, and immature children in Sasur. Though Sasur women have more children, the household is smaller because plural marriage is rare and fewer outsiders are included. These households often suffer internal strain. A Sasur man must have land when he marries; this land is normally some his mother had been cultivating. If she is still actively engaged in farming, this deprives her of some of her resources and satisfactions. Later, when her husband dies, the mother moves into the household with her daughter-in-law. This was the case in 15 percent of the Sasur households. This relationship is frequently a strained one. This source of conflict does not exist in Kapsirika.

A similar strain develops in the case of plural marriages as a result of land ownership patterns in the plantain-growing sector. Sebei men allocate land to their wives in the manner they had traditionally allocated cattle (and still do, where cattle are important). But it is difficult to do this equitably. Tensions between wives and conflicts between the sons of co-wives threaten internal harmony in the households and extended families that arise from this unsatisfactory form of cultural adaptation.

Neighboring households are also more strained. Cattle exchanges between men in Kapsirika create bonds of friendship—or at least continued ties that call for mutual support. Land exchanges between men of Sasur, which they themselves see as having the same character, do not create social bonds. In fact, permanent bonds between Sasur men who are not kin are almost non-existent. The only exception is the beer party—whether as a working *moyket* or as the ritual of *mukutanek*. The *moyket* is, however, essentially a women's affair. Men do participate and occasionally men's work (in conjunction with coffee) is done in collaboration. Nevertheless, Sasur households are more firmly embedded in a context of permanent neighbors. These neighborhood relationships are continuous over long periods, as most men are at least third-generation residents in the community and most of their wives come from Sasur or nearby.

Circumcision Circumcision rites were reshaped to meet the conditions in the two communities. While both retain the rites and in each the youth are generally eager to undergo them, the actual performance is given far greater emphasis in Kapsirika than Sasur. Plains men take pride in making an elaborate and burdensome show of the ritual, while Sasur fathers are all but disinterested. Much of the traditional performance has been lost there.

Circumcision is better attuned to Kapsirikan life because it reinforces the values and behavior requisite to cattle keeping—values that have little relevance to farming. Consider the gifts to initiates. They are far more important in Kapsirika than in Sasur, for they can be more substantial and relevant to be career purposes of the initiation than trinkets or money. Kapsirika boys were regularly given livestock, thus reinforcing the central purpose of their lives and launching their careers as cattlemen. Furthermore, the Kapsirikans could afford to be more generous, for such gifts do not really diminish the household economy since the animals continue to be a part of the herd. There is no comparable gift that a Sasur man can make to his initiate. The values inculcated in the initiation are also appropriate to the cattle raiding and associated military activity in Kapsirika that was forced on them by their aggressive neighbors.

We are therefore not surprised that Kapsirikans take their initiation more seriously than the Sasurese. But this does not account for the lavish and rivalrous display of wealth. I believe this has emerged as a way for the plains men to establish themselves as leaders. Traditional leadership roles were lost with the decline of both age set and clan, so that ownership of cattle came to be the major basis for establishing and demonstrating status. Sasur men of wealth would never engage in elaborate displays of this kind. Perhaps this is because it is more difficult to transform land wealth into consumer goods without at the same time losing capital. Perhaps also the leadership vacuum was not so great, since governmentally appointed chiefs play a far more important role in Sasur than on the plains. Finally, of course, is the basic fact that initiation is no longer integrated into the essential values of the Sasurese.

CONFLICT AND INSTITUTIONAL RESPONSE

Human interaction often creates tensions. These tensions can either be interpersonal or internal to the individual. Jealousy, envy, hatred, and hostility can be disruptive; the preservation of a sense of community calls for institutionalized means to cope with them. Some institutions, such as a court system, are overt patterns for resolving conflict. Others may ameliorate potential conflict by strongly reinforcing a sense of mutual identification. But no society solves all the difficulties that come from the very fact of human social existence, and some people will be resentful or hostile. Such sentiments may be expressed openly or indirectly or even in self-destructive behavior, such as psychological illness or even suicide.

Such negative sentiments are apt to be held by persons who feel that other individuals or groups are depriving them of satisfaction in life. This lowers their feeling of self-worth. Such sentiments are always embedded in the social situation, for both the definition of worth and the means of attaining it are established by the culture. This means that different social contexts evoke different kinds of tension. Remember the shift from *misisi* to *mukutanek*; *misisi* was designed to reduce interpersonal tension between in-laws while *mukutanek* was designed to overcome friction between neighbors.

How do the differing situations in Sasur and Kapsirika alter the points of tension in interpersonal relations? What different means of coping with them have emerged? How has the failure to meet these problems created stress for the individual Sebei in the two communities?

Plural marriages are a potential source of tension. Such tension is not so much a matter of sexual jealousy as we may tend to think, but rather it is derived from issues involving property rights and relative social treatment between the co-wives. Ancient tradition provided the customary procedure for handling the allocation of rights in livestock that could make for equity. The Sebei used these property concepts for the allocation of land. This is an example of cultural continuity that, on its face, seems like a sensible, if not inevitable, solution. But it was fraught with difficulties that could hardly have been anticipated. Cattle are both owned and controlled by men but land is cultivated and managed by women, so there is a separation of the ownership and management roles. With cattle, both ownership and management passes from father to sons; with land, though ownership passes from father to son, the management and use goes from mother to daughter-in-law. Furthermore while a herd can readily be built back up to strength, this is virtually impossible with land.

This leads to conflict between a man's mother and wife. The older woman is often reluctant to give up her land. The two widowed women in Sasur who lived with their sons had more *shambas* than the wives of these men, showing how tenaciously women hold on to their land. In Sebei tradition, the groom's mother is supposed to act as a surrogate mother for a new bride, instructing her in household tasks, but in Sasur there has come to be an informal pattern of mother-in-law avoidance for women—comparable to the traditional avoidance between a man and his mother-in-law. This shows that such tension has developed and that some effort has been made to lessen it.

Land problems also place co-wives in competition. In Sebei tradition, the senior wife (like the mother-in-law) is expected to act as a surrogate mother. But wives are concerned with their own children, most particularly their sons. Sons are expected to take care of their mothers if they become widows after they are too old to be inherited. This gives a woman self-interest in her son's success, even if mother love and pride are not involved.

Sebei men are aware that they must treat their wives equitably. With plentiful land in Kapsirika, men are not worried about access to land and need only to be careful to plow fields of the same size for each wife. It is merely a matter of not showing favoritism in the performance of service. Polygynous Sasur men are aware of potential conflict over land and try to allocate *shambas* equitably, but often find it difficult to do so.

Conflict over land is frequent; we saw this with respect to Psiwa's sons and again in the witchcraft case. The elders there immediately recognized that land allocation was the real source of the conflict between the two women. In contrast, not a single word was spoken about landholdings during the extended discussion over Kambuya's legacy or in the Kapsirika case of witchcraft accusation.

Brothers compete over property among the Sebei, though such conflict runs counter to the Sebei belief that clan brothers must give mutual support. In Kapsirika, conflict is chiefly between full brothers, who divide the cattle that had been anointed for their mother. In Sasur, it is between half brothers, the sons of co-wives, since their access to land will depend upon how it has been allocated to their mothers. This is a continuity of the co-wife conflict. The Sebei do not seem to recognize this source of difficulty, perhaps because it is buried under such a deep layer of convictions about the spiritual demand for fraternal amity. I found no evidence of any ritual or other institutional way of reducing fraternal conflict.

Property Conflicts   Both land and cattle can be stolen. Cattle must be stolen from a distance, preferably by an enemy, for the Sebei recognize each cow and know its owner. It might even merely return to its home of its own accord. But if land is stolen, it will be stolen from a neighbor. The chief methods involve secretly moving the boundary plants between one's own land and one's neighbor's or claiming erroneously that one's neighbor has done so—which amounts to the same thing. Hostility in the agricultural sector is thus directed inward, toward near neighbors, while hostility in Kapsirika is largely directed outward, to alien people. It is not all directed outward (Kilele accused his neighbor of helping the Pokot take his cattle and Kambuya went to court against his son's father-in-law over land), but the constant nagging and inescapable conflict between neighbors found in Sasur does not exist in Kapsirika.

All of these data show that unresolved conflict is greater in Sasur than in Kapsirika. This is because the plains have kept more closely to ancient traditions and their established orderly patterns for conflict resolution. The men and women of the plantain-growing area have adopted new forms of economy and have tried to adapt old institutions to fit. This unresolved conflict in Sasur leads to much unresolved hostility directed both to close kin and fellow villagers.

Unresolved hostility is often expressed in the form of witchcraft and witchcraft accusation. People will resort to witchcraft in situations where they can neither take direct action nor simply move away from their antagonist. We expected to find more expression of witchcraft in Sasur than in Kapsirika, and we did. In the tests administered by Dr. Edgerton, nearly twice as many mentions of witchcraft were made by Sasur respondents than by the Kapsirikans (1.9 per person versus 1.0). When we first arrived in Kapsirika an epidemic of a mild but painful meningitis was under way, yet we heard no suspicion of witchcraft but were asked to help get medical aid. This was in strong contrast to the frequent accusations and rumors of witchcraft in Sasur.

The difference is also apparent in the two cases of witchcraft accusation between co-wives examined in Chapter 5. In the case that took place near Sasur, the two women were in direct confrontation. Though the elders rightly saw the antagonism as an expression of resentment over land, the hatred between the two women was most evident. The accusing wife's description of her encounters with the *oyik* showed her emotionally disturbed condition. The co-wives in the case on the plains expressed neither enmity nor emotional disturbance. Indeed, they gave no evidence of having a quarrel. The cantankerous old mother who was causing the trouble cited as evidence that the co-wife had gone to Sasur, where witches were known to be. The confrontations between Kambuya's sons involved accusations and insinuations about witchcraft, but none of these were taken seriously enough even to raise a direct response. When Kilele suspected his neighbor of helping the raiders, he did not accuse him of witchcraft but called for an oath. All Sebei know about witchcraft, but in Kapsirika they make open accusations that are really name-calling; these do not come out of suppressed hostility but out of anger. The clearest evidence of the difference in the prevalence of witchcraft is that the people of the western escarpment had acquired a new kind of witchcraft, *kankanet*, that was unknown to ancient Sebei and was not found on the plains.

Ethos Witchcraft is an institutionalized means of expressing repressed resentment and anger, but it does not remove these sentiments. They become a part of the underlying ethos of the community. On the basis of his tests and psychological observations, Edgerton drew a picture of Sasur that shows how much these sentiments affect life in the community.

> No one could enter this Sebei world without an immediate awareness of one central feeling tone, felt and seen everywhere. For want of a better word, call it hostility. In some ways, this hostility was visible, as in the

constant gossip, criticism, and corrosive humor of both men and women. These Sebei could also phrase their hostility in an abrasive form of bluster, threat, and posture that was certain to annoy everyone, but was not so extreme that it would lead to open conflict. The Sebei of Sasur avoided open conflict.

Elsewhere Edgerton says:

The Sebei said that they saw every man—and especially every woman— as a potential enemy, a person with the power and the probable intent to destroy crops, to sicken children or cattle, to cause a woman to miscarry, to bring death to an entire family. They lived with fear and tension, and their mistrust of each other was so basic that I sometimes wondered how the tasks of everyday life got done. In fact, the tasks of everyday life were done because mistrust and fear and hatred were kept below the surface, where everyone *could* see them, but no one *had* to see them.

Edgerton continues by pointing out that this inability to express their hostility meant that they had to be devious in their social relationships. He cites the favorite method of seduction as an example.

A man did not ensnare his heart's delight through romantic niceties, nor by acts of derring-do, not even by his family's wealth or his own physical prowess. He did it by filching the beads she wore around her waist. Since a girl could not return home bereft of these beads without calling her chastity into doubt, she would stay with her boyfriend and try to recapture her beads. . . . Men said that they were proud of their ability to trick and coerce women in this way. Women recalled such experiences with anger, speaking of men as "dogs" who would stop at nothing where sex was concerned.

Even direct conflict in Sasur takes an oblique course. Edgerton writes:

An angered Sasur farmer might well choose to burn the house of his enemy, but he would do so at night, when there was no danger of discovery. Even the children I saw avoided the direct fight, and ran away where they pouted and plotted the demise of their enemy. Sasur children did not even fight in play very much.

Finally, Edgerton takes note that this suspicion led to an endemic fear.

Every afternoon . . . I sat, partially obscured, on a large rock that over-looked what took place on a small plateau below me. Scarcely a day passed that I did not see a Sebei man or woman hide behind a bush or tree to watch the activities of some other Sebei. And, sometimes, I saw still another Sebei watching the watcher. . . . This watching was not casual: it was prompted by fear. In characterizing the Sebei of Sasur, I remember a man's typical reaction to my question about whether people were ever so worried that they did not sleep well. He said this: "Who can sleep well? Who does not have worries? Who does not know that someone wants to kill them? No one! Not even a child!"

Edgerton contrasts the behavior on the plains as follows:

I was struck instantly that they did not appear to be living under the cloud of mistrust and fear that covered the farming Sebei. Here, people were not as guarded, not as wary, and not as tense. Here anger did find open expressions as children fought, husbands cuffed their wives, drunken men brawled with each other, and occasionally there was armed combat. . . . Military pride was evident, and men were concerned with strength and courage. Emotion of all sorts was more freely expressed. Anger as well as laughter, despair as well as elation, could be seen on many public occasions. . . .

There was also gloom and sadness, freely expressed, but here they did not result so much from the fear of one's neighbors or relatives as from bad luck, God's will, disease, old age, or the threat of enemy raiders. Even witchcraft, which still occurred, changed its character. Here it was more open, and when it struck, it was more often cattle than humans who were the victims. . . .

There can be no doubt that these people were still Sebei, were still sometimes hostile, reserved, and devious. But they were far less so. I saw no hidden figures watching furtively, and no one told me that even children lived in fear of other Sebei.

Edgerton felt that the Kapsirikans had more pride and a better self-image. He says:

The pastoral Sebei also looked different, for while they will never rival the Pokot pastoralists for sartorial elegance, the men did sport the occasional feather, and women did wear more beads and bracelets than their farming counterparts. Furthermore, each sex ogled each other, and nervously shifted their attire when someone of the opposite sex happened by. These pastoralist women were much more lusty and provocative than their farming counterparts.

ANOMIE AND THE EVOLUTIONARY PROCESS

The ex-Chief Junusu Wandera once said to me "The Sebei are easy to be converted to new fashions." That is in fact the case. Their close relatives the Pokot and their northern neighbors the Karamojong to this day retain much of their traditional dress, economy, and ritual. The more distantly related Maasai, whose territory is close to Nairobi, the largest city in East Africa, also retain in remarkable degree their ancient traditions and patterns of life, despite the efforts of colonial officers, missionaries, and the governments of Kenya and Tanzania. By contrast, Sebei is far more remote and less affected by these external forces, yet far more changed.

This readiness to change indicates a lack of commitment to the values of the traditional culture. This indifference indicates the failure of a sense of purpose. This failure cannot be blamed on colonial rule for it had become part of the culture that existed when the British arrived. Evidence for this includes Sebei failure in military action. This inability to resist effectively depredation by neighbors suggests a failure of will rather than weakness in numbers or strategic vulnerability. This lack of will is also known by the character of their major ceremonies for *poroyet* and clan, which never give voice to their strength, unity, and virtue nor raise membership loyalty as an ideal. This lack of commitment remains and is expressed in the psychological testing performed by Dr. Edgerton. The answers given by a cohesive group will tend to cluster around recognized values; Sebei responses showed great variation and little clustering.

Both Edgerton's description of suspiciousness and hostility, especially in Sasur, which was further removed from traditional practices, and the tests administered to them revealed the Sebei as being generically anxious and almost obsessed with the fear of death. These fears are old, for they are expressed in their traditional rites.

Sebei anomie, their ease in being converted to new fashions, is a consequence of rapid change. Customs, values, and religious institutions have the power to reinforce the kind of behavior needed to maintain the community, even behavior that is dangerous, difficult, or merely irksome. But these reinforcements are inappropriate to the new behavioral expectations that result from changed conditions. Thus, initiation rites are highly appropriate inducements to raiding, but not to the pursuit of horticulture. Such inappropriateness applies to small as well as major matters. Thus, Sasur parents, just like those of Kapsirika, said that the first thing a boy should learn was to herd sheep and goats, though most of them had no such animals, and none of the boys would become herdsmen. While it is easy to see that a new resource (for instance, cultivating plantains) is worth exploiting and hence changing activities accordingly, it is not easy to see the social consequences of such change (for instance, the altered character of military action). Yet ultimately these changed patterns became institutionalized. It is even more difficult for a people to see the psychological effects that these new institutional forms induce (for instance, the problems inherent in transforming cattle law into land law) and yet harder still for them to find an institutionl solution to these issues. At the very least, finding solutions takes time.

The transformations that took place on Mount Elgon in the eighteenth and nineteenth centuries were massive; the Sebei had started to find ways of coping with new social practices. But they did not have enough time to achieve a new harmony when another, even more overpowering force for change hit them. While one can never know what would have happened had circumstances been different, I believe that one of two things would have occurred on the north slopes of Mount Elgon by now had there been no colonialism: either they would have developed a strong community based and ritually reinforced social system, or they would have been annihilated. As it happened, the Sebei were caught in a state of flux.

A MODEL FOR EVOLUTIONARY CHANGE

We have seen both change and diversity in Sebei patterns of behavior: institutions disappear (harvest rituals) or lose their central purpose and hence much of their structure (age sets) or are reformulated to meet new exigencies (*misisi/mukutanek*) or transformed to new purposes (cattle rights to land

TABLE 1   DIAGRAMMATIC SUMMARY OF THE PROCESS OF ADAPTATION IN SEBEI

Item	Historic		Comparative	
	OLD	NEW	KAPSIRIKA	SASUR
Ecological condition	Semiarid plains	Wet mountainside; Protection from raids	Semiarid plains; Enemies close	Wet mountainside; Enemies distant
Economic choice	Primarily cattle	Primarily horticulture	Primarily cattle	Horticulture, especially plantains
Direct consequences				
Settlement	Age-based *manyattas*	Dispersed on land	Widely dispersed	Highly concentrated
Warfare	Cattle raiding	Defensive	Defensive raiding	No warfare
Land control	All land public	Much land private	Land freely available	Land hard to get
Institutional response				
Age sets	Primary institution with internal structure	Military and political functions lost; no structure	Unimportant	Unimportant
Initiation group	?	*Poroyet* based	Local but elaborate	Local; deemphasized
Territorial units	Probably slight	*Poroyet*	Subordinated to political system	Subordinated to political system
Clan	Basis for legal action	Increase in function, later decline	No legal function; Oathing only	No legal function; Oathing only
Legal decision	Clan and seniority	Community (*chomi ntarasiit*)	Colonial political system	Colonial political system
Leadership roles	Age-set based	Personal based	Rich cattlemen	Political officials
Marriage for men	Long delayed	Early marriage	Polygyny frequent	Polygyny rare
Brideprice	—	—	Higher	Lower
Stress loci	Affinal kin	Neighbors	Other tribes; Full brothers	Neighbors; Half-brothers; Co-wives; Mother/daughter-in-law

	Misisi	Mukutanek		
Institutional response			Military preparation Equitable land preparation Public confrontation	No military Formal land distribution Witchcraft confrontation (*kankanet*)
Psychological character				
Community life	?	Ritually reinforced but treated negatively	Some informal community involvement	No community involvement
Interpersonal relationships	?	Diffuse anxiety	Confrontational but not fearful (depression)	Rampant fear and distrust

rights). We have seen new institutions adopted from outside (*kankanet* witchcraft) or created on the spot (*chomi ntarastit*). We have seen institutions differently treated under different circumstances (circumcision feasts in Sasur and Kapsirika). Finally, we have seen that these different patterns of social life have altered the sentiments and feelings of the people by creating different kinds of tension and concern. Can we make any generalizations about the nature of changes and thus help to explain the process of evolutionary adaptation?

I believe there is an orderliness to this process. We must first examine some general principles. First, we must state the obvious: change follows from a *preexisting condition*. An orderly system of behavior, expectations, and institutions always has been in existence before the alterations took place. These had themselves been adaptations to the then existing situation.

Second, change takes place because of some altered circumstance in the relationship between the people and their environment. This may be an altered environment (as in migration to a new area) or an altered means of exploiting that environment (whether invented or borrowed). It may also be the appearance of new neighbors, who may alter the broader context within which the society exists. Any of these may constitute an *exogenic force* and may be seen as the *cause* of evolutionary change.

Third, such exogenic forces *alter the options* for action in the sense that they create new opportunities, different evaluations of existing courses of action, and different hazards and payoffs for such courses of action.

Fourth, change occurs when individuals take a new course of action in response to their reevaluation of these altered opportunities and the perception of their own self-interest. It is useful to think of individuals as the *agents* of change.

Fifth, because people are raised in an ongoing system with its established values and expectations, individuals will minimize the degree to which they alter their behavior and will try to compromise between the new and old. This may be called *cultural inertia*. This means that when new patterns emerge, they will utilize insofar as possible the prexisting forms.

Sixth, individuals engaging in such action do not see themselves as changing society or culture; they do not and cannot know the consequences of the actions they take. Yet it is these *unanticipated consequences* that constitute the evolutionary process in culture.

Seventh, these consequences may satisfy the new condition, but they often create further problems. When this is the case, it affects peoples' behavior and creates a new basis for further change.

Such a continuing cycle of cause and effect should theoretically end in a new stability. But such a situation is rarely likely to be found before new exogenic forces create new conditions, new options, and new solutions, and so on.

In Table 1 I have tried to summarize social change as it has applied to the Sebei data, placing information on the historical change side by side with the comparative data.

CHANGE AS THE HUMAN CONDITION

Most anthropological studies emphasize stability and speak of equilibrium and homeostasis; the general presupposition is that tribal peoples' lives are unchanging. The fact is that change must be viewed as the normal condition of human existence. If one stops to contemplate the 50 or more thousand years that our own subspecies *Homo sapiens sapiens* has lived on the earth, has moved to the hottest of deserts and to the frozen arctic, has reached high up the sides of mountains and deep into the jungles; and when one further contemplates the vast array of tools and technologies that have been accumulated to exploit these diverse environments, then one certainly must recognize that change, rather than stability, is the nature of the human condition. This change has been evolutionary in the grand sense; it has seen the accumulation of knowledge, the increased complexity of the social lives of the people, and the great diversity in their forms.

This growth of civilization, as we like to call it, is the outcome of the actions of individuals, millions upon millions of actions by millions upon millions of people, responding to new opportunities and in the process creating for themselves new sources of tension and concern that in turn they must find means to ameliorate. It is a process of challenge and response; but it is also a process laden with difficulties. The Sebei have given us a glimpse into what this process is like.

Epilogue

The colonial era ended in Uganda in 1962. That year the British ended the Uganda Protectorate and the nation of Uganda was established. There were, of course, the usual independence celebrations, locally and nationally. We remained in Kapsirika, where the men anticipated that the Pokot from across the Kenya border would initiate raids, taking advantage of the distraction caused by the celebration. They were not disappointed, though the raid was a small one, emptying the *kraal* belonging to Kilele..

The Sebei had begun to anticipate *uhuru*, as independence is called in Swahili, by establishing their own independence. For most of the colonial era, Sebei was a part of a district dominated by the Gisu, the very people who had driven them out of part of their territory. The Gisu and the Sebei no longer fought battles in the field, but they were constantly warring in matters of policy. In this the Gisu were also at an advantage; they were closer to the seat of government, as the district office was in their territory; they were more numerous, and more prosperous as well; they had more educated men and women, and they had more people working in the government in positions of authority. The Gisu did many things and passed many rules that went against Sebei custom and deprived the Sebei of property and opportunity. Some Sebei leaders made an open confrontation that led the Protectorate government to establish Sebei as a separate district with its own district commissioner—Aloni Muzungyu, who had long been chief. They also had a very astute young politician who was an influential member of the parliament of the Protectorate.

Despite this conflict, many Gisu lived in Sebei territory. Some Gisu men had bought land from Sebei; many Gisu women had married Sebei men. The relationships between ordinary people seem generally to have been cordial. All in all, the Sebei looked forward to the postcolonial era with optimism as they moved toward greater involvement with modern politics.

The subsequent years have not, however, been kind to them. The national government was dominated by tribal factionalism and when Milton Obote was elected president he exiled the *kabaka* (king of the Baganda, the largest ethnic group in the nation). Under his regime cattle raiding in the plains escalated from that small beginning at the time of the *uhuru* celebrations to

151

large-scale attacks. As a result, most of the plains, including Kapsirika, had been emptied of people and the dry bush returned to the nurture of giraffe, zebra, and antelope. The contest between Salimu, Ndiwa, and Andyema over Kambuya's cattle had in the end proved fruitless to all.

The disaffection of the Baganda brought on a coup by an army officer, Idi Amin, who started a dictatorial rule of violence. It also brought corruption. One of my Sebei friends wrote in 1983 that corruption had "become the drama of the day" and that "you can hardly get service of any kind from an officer or chief without the release of cash."

Our last visit among the Sebei was made in 1972. There had been some material improvement. Kapchorwa, the district headquarters, had electricity and telephone service. A secondary school had been established on the road between our old village of Sasur and Kapchorwa. We found lodging there in quarters left by American Peace Corps volunteers who had been withdrawn from service in Uganda after a corpsman (in another part of Uganda) had been killed.

Amin himself visited Sebei while we were there. He arrived in a helicopter out of a stormy sky; after a delay caused by rain he gave a long lecture to the group assembled on the playing field, and then joined briefly in native dances, before he flew off into the threatening sky. He gave every evidence of being a man of the people.

But his legacy was one of destruction. He appointed an army officer from a distant tribe as district commissioner. Sebei leaders were imprisoned or disappeared. One Sebei who had been jailed and escaped told stories of torture and murder. Sebei leaders, never very relaxed, seemed tense and uncertain. One young man decided we were dangerous when we took the old familiar road to Kapsirika and Greek River and insisted on accompanying us. He was disappointed when, at Greek River, we were invited by Kali Kali, the district commissioner, to join him for a beer. One of my assistants on an errand to Mbale, the nearest city, found himself in the midst of army shooting and wisely left.

Economic conditions declined because of governmental policies. The hoarding of goods by the wealthy and powerful left ordinary people destitute and many Sebei "have resorted to smuggling as a means of earning a living," my friend wrote. The poverty has, he goes on to say, "exposed the Sebei to nutritional diseases like pellagra." Coffee marketing became difficult except by smuggling across the Suam River into Kenya. The price of staples such as kerosene, sugar, and tea skyrocketed. Jobs were hard to get.

Other changes struck us as important. Amin, coming from a tribe that spoke neither Swahili nor Luganda, the official language of the country, ordered elementary schools to teach in English. So the young children were speaking English, which their parents could not understand. It made the children arrogant and unruly. However, this had had the effect of increased interest in education, and more parents began sending their children to school. When possible, they send them to Kenya, because Uganda has a shortage of teachers.

The consumption of alcohol had increased measurably. Beer was a part of their ancient tradition. The use had already been great and by 1962 a good deal of it was converted on native stills into a potent and usually unappetizing *waragi* or gin. But while there was incessant social drinking and an occasional old man weaving his way down the road, abusive drunkenness was rarely encountered. By 1972 this had changed. The circumcision we attended was no longer the jolly, somewhat tipsy and ribald affair, but was more like a drunken brawl with a good deal of fighting. For the first time in my long involvement with the Sebei, I encountered hostility.

Another change, reported in my friend's letter, was that "ethnic differences between the Sebei and the Gisu took root. This resulted in the expulsion of the Gisu from Sebeiland. The Sebei saw the opportunity to acquire evacuated land, thus easing the effects of increasing population."

These events can best be conveyed by sharing a letter from a young woman of Sebei, who wrote in 1979, shortly after Amin was driven from office.

> Try to imagine the remains of a murderous dictatorship as that of Amin. Some sense of development had started seeping in during the late sixties until Amin took over. Then things started to fall. Agriculture was worst hit. Sebei was totally forgotten on the side of machinery, yet Amin and his henchmen expected wheat and maize from poor Sebei. If it were not for our dear donkey and a tractor here and there, I don't know what would have become of our people.

She continued by saying that the road across the escarpment "is no better than a cattle track, since the Ministry of Works forgot its duty immediately after Amin took over." She also noted that the people of Benet are cutting down the forest. Then she told us what happened after Amin was overthrown.

> In May of this year [1979], what I would call a revolution took place in Sebei. Because of the terrible conditions during Amin's time, people moved about in all directions in search of better conditions. The Gisu would bring coffee from their homes to the Suam River and other border areas to exchange for Kenya currency. Of the many who came, a certain number remained in order to be near the border and others settled throughout Sebei.
>
> On Amin's fall, the Sebei went wild. Practically every Gisu was an enemy. So many were killed, property was looted, children got lost. A small child of five years, or three, or six would be found miles and miles from where they had been with their parents, without knowing where their parents were, or the parents knowing where they are. Some met with their children after months, after all hope had been lost.
>
> A few Sebei families played the role of savior—hiding the Gisu from the cruel guns left by Amin's army and from looting and from arrows. At my father's home, Gisu filled the rooms—two bedrooms and the sitting room. Nobody would go out. "Short calls" were released in basins for almost a full week, with guns booming from morning to evening. Many who came back to sell land put up in my father's house.
>
> Many of Amin's henchmen who had brought terror to many people in Sebei—raping mercilessly, wanton killing irrespective of age, etc. etc.— were rushed down the hills and gutted with gun barrels or shot to death. The Lugbara from Amin's West Nile had it hot!

She goes on to indicate that the availability of firearms altered the balance of power on the plains, at least temporarily.

The Karamojong and Pokot still come to raid us, but they can't match the Sebei now. Amin let his guns loose and many Sebei boys took advantage of this. They simply go down to Pokot land and swipe many head of cattle just for the sake of those Sebei who were killed in great numbers and for the looted property and burned houses. When the boys remember all this they just go mad. The Pokot have now moved far away from the border.

So old enmities take new forms as the new technology transforms both drinking and fighting. Subsequent letters indicate that the fighting has abated, but that the Sebei continue to suffer economic hardship and political deprivation. However, they are now firmly in the modern world, and the solutions to their problems will have to be made within the context that, for better or for worse, the Western world has provided.

Readings

Edgerton, Robert B., 1971, *The Individual in Cultural Adaptation: A Study of Four East African Peoples*. Berkeley and Los Angeles, University of California Press.
This volume examines in detail the sociopsychological character of farming and pastoral communities among the Kamba, Hehe, Pokot, and Sebei, using a variety of test instruments, including a specially designed picture test of values.

Goldschmidt, Walter, 1959, *Man's Way: A Preface to the Understanding of Human Society*. New York, Holt, Rinehart and Winston.
An essay on the evolution of culture in relation to the behavioral characteristics of human sociality.

———, 1966, *Sebei Law*, Berkeley and Los Angeles, University of California Press.
A detailed examination of the legal aspect of Sebei traditional culture.

———, 1967, *Kambuya's Cattle: The Legacy of an African Herdsman*, Berkeley and Los Angeles, University of California Press.
The record of the hearing on the estate of Kambuya and also of Tengedyes's accusation of witchcraft.

———, 1976, *The Culture and Behavior of the Sebei: A Study in Continuity and Adaptation* (with the assistance of Gale Goldschmidt). Berkeley and Los Angeles, University of California Press.
A detailed account of Sebei culture, both traditional and current.

Sahlins, Marshall D. and Elman R. Service (eds.), 1960, *Evolution and Culture*. Ann Arbor, University of Michigan Press.
A major work expressing the modern neo-evolutionary approach to culture with an important distinction between general (Grand Scheme) and specific (ecological) orientations to evolution.

Steward, Julian H. 1977, in *Evolution and Ecology: Essays on Social Transformation* (Jane C. Steward and Robert F. Murphy, eds.), Urbana, University of Illinois Press.
A posthumous publication of essays by the pioneer in the development of an ecological approach to the understanding of cultural development.

Glossary

This glossary includes technical words and terms that have been used in special ways in this work as well as Sebei words. Native words are printed in italics; they are Sebei unless specifically identified otherwise. The list also includes the names of tribes referenced in the book.

acculturation: The process of adopting elements of a dominant culture by a tribal or subordinate group.

age grade: A status and set of behavioral expectations based upon age and sex.

age set: A social unit, one of a cycle or series of such units, in which membership is based on age, and is usually established through initiation at or about puberty.

agriculture: The cultivation of plants with the use of the plow, as distinct from horticulture, which uses the hoe or other hand tools.

aret (*arosiek*, pl.): A patrilineal clan. Literally, path.

Baganda: A Bantu-speaking people living on the north shore of Lake Victoria whose kingdom (Buganda) had extensive control. It was the Baganda who first subjected the Sebei to colonial rule.

blocked arrow: An arrow head with a transverse blade for making a cut rather than a point; used for bleeding cattle.

brideprice: The payment of goods and valuables by the groom or his family to the family of the bride. It may be a standard prestation or closely haggled over. It is not to be confused with a dowry, which is wealth given (usually by the bride's family) to the couple being married.

bull-roarer: A widely used instrument in association with rituals. It consists of a blade-shaped piece of wood attached to a string that makes a deep roaring sound when whirled.

career: The life pattern of an individual in the pursuit of both physical needs and social satisfaction, in accordance with the expectations of the community.

chemeryantet (*chemerik*, pl.): A person undergoing his or her initiation.

chomi ntarastit: A ritual initiated by the prophet Matui that was essentially an oath of allegiance and a recognition of the right of the community to punish any offense such as murder or theft.

chyme: The partially digested content of the stomach.

clan: A kin group based upon unilineal descent (either matrilineal or patrilineal) whose members consider themselves to be related, but who cannot actually trace their kinship. (See *aret*.)

colonialism: The control of native or local population by outside (usually

157

European) nations, which impose their control over these populations for their own purposes. The colonial period in Sebei began in 1899 and ended in 1962.

cultigens: Domesticated plants.

Cushitic: A language family centered in Ethiopa and by extension the people speaking one of these languages. It is believed that Cushitic people once were widespread throughout East Africa, of which only remnants are left.

Dorobo: A term applied to hunting and gathering peoples found in East Africa.

Gisu: A Bantu-speaking tribe living on the western slope of Mount Elgon and on the plains below it to the west.

heifer: A female calf, before she matures and can be serviced.

horticulture: The cultivation of plants with the use of the hoe or other hand tools, as distinct from agriculture.

kankanet: A form of witchcraft introduced into the western sector of the Sebei that affects only a guilty person.

kaporet: The senior person of a group of youths undergoing initiation together. Seniority is calculated by the seniority of the fathers.

Karamojong: A Nilotic people living on the plains north of the Sebei.

kintet: The bull of the herd; an animal that is especially prized and is a kind of alter ego to the owner.

kirkitaptoka: See *kintet*.

kokwet: Council or council place.

korosek: A group of plants that are thought to be health-giving or cleansing substances, used in certain ceremonies and by extension those rites that utilized these plants.

kota (*korik*, pl.):   A patrilineal lineage. Literally, house. Also used for lines of cattle.

kraal: An Afrikaans word meaning corral, an enclosure for livestock.

lineage: A descent group in which individuals can actually calculate their relationship. May be either patrilineal or matrilineal (see *kota*.)

Maasai: A Southern Nilotic pastoralist people living in Kenya and Tanzania.

manyatta: A Swahili word for homestead or group of homesteads enclosed by a brush fence.

Masop: Mount Elgon. Also the personified ancestor of the Sebei. The Sebei also use the word to mean up the mountain, so that the people of Sasur are referred to as "in *masop*" by the people of the plains.

Mbai: The westernmost of the three tribes that make up modern Sebei. Sasur is in Mbai territory.

misisi: A traditional ritual of thanksgiving in which the host invites specified kindred.

motoriyontet: The instructor or sponsor of an initiate.

moyket: A work party, in which the family for whom the work is done provides beer (and under certain circumstances also food).

mukutanek: A ritual beer party to which the host invites neighbors: a ritual that evolved out of *misisi*.

mumek, mumyantet: A form of witchcraft.

mwet (*mwenik*, pl.):   A child serving as caretaker, usually of younger children, but also applied to children who take care of initiates or brides during their period of seclusion.

namanya: A contractural relationship between two persons in which one man furnishes a bullock in return for a future cow by taking a heifer until she has produced a female calf, which he keeps. The relationship is also used for other exchanges with delayed payoff.

Nandi: A people speaking a language closely related to the Sebei and living to the south of Mount Elgon in Kenya.

nomadism: A pattern of life in which the people move their residence from one place to another within a defined territory in order to pursue their economic activities. Pastoralists are in varying degrees nomadic.

oynatet (*oyik*, pl.):   Spirit of the dead.

panet: A form of witchcraft.

panga: Swahili word for bush knife or machete.

pastoralism: A type of production economy found in the more arid portions of the world in which production centers on the keeping of livestock that utilize natural vegetation. Pastoralists may in varying degrees also engage in farming, but may be considered pastoralist when their life-styles are dominated by the needs of the livestock.

picture test: A test devised by Edgerton and Goldschmidt to elicit statements of value and choice in set events. The test consists of a set of drawings of scenes used to evoke responses.

plantains: Bananas that are used as a staple food and must be cooked before eaten.

Pokot: A people living to the northeast of the Sebei speaking a closely related language.

polygyny: The custom of men taking more than one wife.

pororyet: A county or parish; the smallest geographical entity for which Sebei membership was formalized. Originally meant a batallion.

prestation: An obligatory gift; a transfer of goods that is somewhere between being freely given and paid as a legal obligation.

prophet: A man who has the supernatural ability to foresee events and is sought out before any major undertaking.

reciprocity: The pattern of returning favors rather than making an effort to exploit a relationship.

rite of passage: A ritual that transforms a person from one status to another.

Sabaot: The cluster of tribes that lived on the slopes of Mount Elgon, including the Sebei.

sangta: A village. Original meaning was the place where people of the household or larger community gathered for discussions.

Sapiñ: The easternmost of the three tribes that make up modern Sebei.

senchontet: A long-lived plant (*Dracaena deremensis* Engl.) used as a boundary marker.

shamba: Swahili word meaning a hoe-cultivated garden plot.

Sor: The central one of the three tribes that make up modern Sebei.

Southern Nilotic: People speaking related languages living in East Africa, to which the Sebei belong. They are in varying degrees pastoralists.

Swahili: A people living on the coast of Kenya who were involved in the trade with the interior of Africa prior to colonialism, and who penetrated Sebei territory before the appearance of Europeans.

tekeryontet: A twin, a person born after twins, a breech-born person, and others who by circumstances of their birth are viewed as special and vulnerable.

tekonymy: The practice of calling a woman by a name derived from her child; that is, "mother of ———."

Teso: A Nilotic people living on the plains to the west and northwest of Sebei.

tilyet: Individuals who have engaged in a *namanya exchange*. They address one another as *tilyenyu* (my cattle kin) and are expected to maintain amicable relationships.

tokapsoi: The cattle belonging to a man that he has not allocated to any of his wives but kept for his own free use.

waragi: A Swahili word for native-made distillate of beer; gin.

warek: A word for sheep and goats combined.

wergild: The payment of compensation by the guilty group for a murder of a man of another group.

Index

Adaptation, 129–149
  ecological, 134–137
  natural, 133
  prehistoric, 130–132
  ritual, 52–61
  secondary consequences of, 130
Adultery, 127–128
Age grades, 21
Age-set system, 2, 21–25, 26, 29, 30, 108, 125, 131
Agricultural rites, 123
Agriculture, 13, 27, 32, 73, 133, 153
  See also Farming
Amin, Idi, 6, 152, 153, 154
Animal husbandry, 13–25, 135
Anomie, 144–145
Anxiety, 127, 145
Arkok, cave of, 7
Austin, Herbert H., 36
Authority, 131, 132

Baganda (people), 63, 152
Bagwere (people), 115
Beer making, 2, 10, 44
Beer parties, 44–47, 139
Benet (village), 7, 10, 27, 153
Binyinyi (village), 7, 39
Blood, cattle, 1, 76
Bride capture, 56
Bride payments, 2, 18, 48, 56–61
Buganda, 36
Bukwa (town), 7, 8, 21
Bulegene (village), 3, 22
Bull-roarers, 105–106
Burial practices, 66–67

Careers, 135–137
  changing patterns of, 34
Cattle, 1, 2, 7, 14, 71, 74–80
  funeral negotiations and, 80–89
  marriage and, 18–19
  social uses of, 78–80
Cattle contracts, 19–21, 44, 76–80
Cattle exchanges, 76–80, 139
Cattle inheritance ritual, 122–123
Change, process of, 129–149
Child rearing, 54
Children, rites for, 117–118, 123
Chomi ntarastit, 30–31
Circumcision, 2, 14, 22–25, 95–111, 125, 132, 139–140
Civilization, growth of, 149
Clan meeting, 116–117
Clans, 2, 16–18, 26, 33, 116–117, 125, 131
Clitoridectomy, 2, 22

Coffee, 10, 37, 41, 43, 135
Cohen, Sir Andrew, 7, 39
Colonialism, 34, 36–37
  changes and, 132–134
  end of, in Uganda, 151
Conflicts, coping with, 140–144
Copper, use of, 2
Corn, 10, 71
Corruption, 152
Court system, 133
Cowrie shells, 2, 118
Crops, 1, 10, 11, 41, 73
Cultural heritage, 13–26
Cultural inertia, 146
Curses, 116–117, 124
  removal of, 63–65

Death, 66–69, 72
  fear of, 41, 127, 145
Disease, see Illness
Disease ritual, 115
Divination, 72–73, 117, 123
Diviners, 62–63
Domestic rites, 122–123
Dorobo (people), 2, 27

Ecological adaptations, 134–137
Ecology, basic changes in, 10–11
Economy
  basic, 1, 13–16
  changes in, 10–11
Edgerton, Robert B., 40, 94, 111, 127, 142, 143, 145
Education, 152
Ethos, Sebei, 126–128, 142–144
Exogamy, 18

Family relationships, 54–55
Farming, 27–28, 39, 71, 130, 131
  See also Agriculture
Fear, 143–144, 145
Fulbright, J. William, 39
Funerals, 66–69
  livestock negotiations at, 80–89

Gisu (tribe), 3, 11, 33, 48, 91, 151, 153
Glossary, 157–160
Goats, 1, 7, 14
Goldschmidt, Gale, 39, 40, 66, 96
Goldschmidt, Mark, 39
Grain, 1, 2, 10, 73
Greek River, 8, 71, 72, 152

Harvest ritual, 114–115, 127
Hazing, 2, 23–24, 105–106

Honey, 2, 10
Hostility, 127, 142–144, 145, 153
Households, 138–139
Hupa Indians (California), 130

Illness, 62–66, 72
Initiation, 2, 21–25, 30, 96–97, 139
Institutionalization, 130, 134
Iron, use of, 2, 13

Jealousy, 127
Juba expedition, 34, 36

Kabruron (village), 7
Kakunguru, Semai, 36
Kalenjin language group, 1
Kali Kali, 7, 152
Kapchorwa (village), 6, 152
Kapsirika (village), 8, 9, 39, 40, 71–94, 134–
    137, 152
    community attitude in, 93–94
Karamojong (people), 8, 11, 71, 72, 135,
    144, 154
Kinship, 16–18, 26
Kipsigi (people), 1
Korosek rites, 114–115

Land, 1–11
    as property, 32–34
    attitude toward, 26
    in Sasur, 48–52
Land ownership, 131–132
Language, 1
Law
    community, 31–32
    traditional, 30–31
Livestock, 1, 2, 10, 13, 71, 74–80, 135
    social relationships and, 18–25, 26
    symbol of wealth, 16, 26
Location of Sebei tribe, 1

Maasai (people), 1, 11, 24, 144
Manyatta, 25–26, 28, 134
Marriage, 18, 20, 55–61, 122, 132, 138
    cattle and, 18–19
Maunya arap Salimu, 5, 6, 40
Mbai (tribe), 3, 28, 40
Milk, 1, 76
Misisi, 52–54, 126, 132, 140
Missionaries, 133–134
Money, 133
Mount Debasien, 8
Mount Elgon, 1, 3, 10, 11, 27, 48, 113
Mourning rites, 68
Moykets, 44–47, 74, 137, 139
Mukutanek, 52, 54, 126, 132, 139, 140
Muzungyu, Aloni, 33, 151

Nandi (people), 1, 11
Ndembu (people), 121
Nomadism, 1
Nyelit (village), 134

Oaths, 31–32, 65, 94, 116, 117, 124, 126,
    131, 133
Obote, Milton, 151

Pastoral tradition, 1–3
Patrilineal descent groups, 2, 16–18
Plantain ritual, 115–116
Plantains, 10–11, 40, 41, 131, 135
Pokot (people), 1, 8, 11, 71, 93, 135, 144,
    151, 154
Polygamy, 2, 41, 73, 91, 138, 140
Pororyet, 28, 29, 91, 125–126, 130–131
Porter, Philip W., 40, 48
Prestation, 18, 60
Prophets, 17, 21, 114, 118, 131
    elimination of, 36, 125

Raiding, 2, 11, 16, 28, 91–93
Rainfall, 10, 27, 135
Reciprocity, 44
Religion, 113–128
Research program, 39–41
Rites of passage, 22, 117, 121–122
Ritual adaptation, 52–61
Rituals, 114–127, 131
Roscoe, John, 39

Sangta, 28, 29
Sapiñ (tribe), 3, 29
Sasur (village), 5, 39–69, 73, 134–137
    land in, 48–52
Sedentarization, 27–29
Seduction, method of, 143
Sheep, 1, 10, 14
Siblings, relationship between, 54–55
Sipi (town), 4, 39, 40, 41
Sipi River, 4–5
Smuggling, 152
Social class, 33
Social system, 2, 11, 16–18
Society, Sebei, transformation of, 27–37
Sor (tribe), 3, 29
Sorcery, see Witchcraft
Southern Nilotic peoples, 1
Spirits, 114, 126

Tekeryontet, 117–118
Tensions, coping with, 140–144
Territorial organization, 25–26, 28
Teso (people), 11, 115
Tribe, concept of, 25, 28–29
Turner, Victor, 121
Twins, ritual upon birth of, 117, 118–121

Uganda, independence of, 132, 151

Wandera, Junusu, 144
Waragi (gin), 153
Warfare, 2, 16, 28, 91–93, 130–131
    effect of, 11
    modern, 92–93
    organization of, 29–30
    traditional, 91–92
Wealth, 15–16
Wedding rites, 60, 126
Witchcraft, 63, 65–66, 117, 124, 136, 142,
    144
    family relations and, 89–91
Women, status of, 16, 32, 42, 137